BIBLICAL
imagination
SERIES

MARK

The Gospel of Passion

MICHAEL CARD

IVP Books

An imprint of InterVarsity Press
Downers Grove, Illinois

InterVarsity Press
P.O. Box 1400, Downers Grove, IL 60515-1426
World Wide Web: www.ivpress.com
E-mail: email@ivpress.com

InterVarsity Press® is the book-publishing division of InterVarsity Christian Fellowship/USA®, a movement of
students and faculty active on campus at hundreds of universities, colleges and schools of nursing in the United States
of America, and a member movement of the International Fellowship of Evangelical Students. For information
about local and regional activities, write Public Relations Dept., InterVarsity Christian Fellowship/USA, 6400
Schroeder Rd., P.O. Box 7895, Madison, WI 53707-7895, or visit the IVCF website at <www.intervarsity.org>.

Cover design: Cindy Kiple
Interior design: Beth Hagenberg
Images: Lowering of the paralytic from the roof. The Four Gospels, Mount Athos Monastery, Iberon, Greece at
    National Library, Athens, Greece. Erich Lessing Art Resource, NY

ISBN 978-0-8308-3813-4

Printed in the United States of America ∞

Library of Congress Cataloging-in-Publication Data

Card, Michael, 1957-
    Mark: the gospel of passion/Michael Card.
        p. cm.
    Includes bibliographical references (p.   ).
    ISBN 978-0-8308-3813-4 (pbk.: alk. paper)
    1. Bible. N.T. Mark—Criticism, interpretation, etc.   I. Title.
    BS2585.52.C368 2011
    226.3'077—dc23

2011047333

| **P** | 20 | 19 | 18 | 17 | 16 | 15 | 14 | 13 | 12 | 11 | 10 | 9 | 8 | 7 | 6 |
| **Y** | 29 | 28 | 27 | 26 | 25 | 24 | 23 | 22 | 21 | 20 | 19 | | | | |

Dedication to William Lane

For more than thirty years I have lived proudly in the shadow of William Lane. As much as any human being can owe another I owe to Bill, who poured his life into me. I trust he would have approved of this book on Mark, though perhaps he might not have agreed with all of it. In this series, I propose to carry on his method of "engaging with the text of Scripture at the level of the informed imagination."

His commentary on the Gospel of Mark is recognized as the best work of its kind in the English language, so it is with a measure of fear and trembling that I approach the task. I believe he would be most honored if I avoided merely regurgitating what I learned from him and tried in a small way to advance some new ideas. So this small effort is dedicated to you, Bill, with deep gratitude for putting the pieces of my life together, for pouring your best self in to me for twenty-six years. Thousands of your students still miss you every single day.

May the Lord receive glory from this gift to the church.

Michael Card, Chang Mai, Thailand

Bill's inscription in my copy of his Mark commentary, dated 1978:

Mike:

I appreciate deeply the privilege of having been able to work with you on the text of Scripture. You know how important it is to develop a listening stance, as one who needs to be made wise by the wisdom of God. As I listened to Mark I heard the call to service, that Jesus, the servant Lord, may become visible within a world that desires to be served. I welcome your participation with me in the order of service to which we have been called by our Lord.

With respect and affection,

William L. Lane

Mark 10:42–45

Less than a year before his death, on July 31, 1998, seeing his commentary sitting on my shelf, Bill asked if he could re-sign it:

Michael:

I couldn't help but notice how our relationship some twenty years ago was not nearly as close as it has become. Which one of us could have guessed what riches the Lord would lavish upon us over the course of more than two decades! I thank God for you, and for all we have shared and continue to share, by way of our ever-deepening friendship, mutual respect and shared awe in the presence of our majestic God. What joy to be able to share from the Gospel of Mark with you and Susan and the children in the front row.

With deepest appreciation and a brother's love,

Bill

CONTENTS

THE BIBLICAL IMAGINATION

"Follow Me," Jesus told them,
"and I will make you fish for people!"

MARK 1:17

Of all the mysterious moments, he seems most approachable at this particular one, most inviting, most available, most human. We imagine the would-be disciples looking up from their nets and fish, smiling at Jesus' creative figure of speech. It is a warm Galilee spring day. It is silent; not even the sound of a bird can be heard. The sand is warm between the fishermen's toes. It is an inviting moment, almost cozy.

You and I have imagined this scene during a hundred sermons. The excitement of the disciples' hearts resonates in ours. If we had been there on that A.D. 29 morning, we would have left everything too. If, like me, this is how you first imagined that long-ago moment, then, like me—you would have been completely wrong.

"We imagine." What do we mean when we say those words? More importantly, what are we really doing when we imagine? As created beings, one of our greatest treasures, perhaps the dearest fingerprint of God on us, is our ability to imagine. But inevitably, whenever I speak about the "biblical imagination" someone will object, "Isn't the imagination a bad thing? Doesn't the Bible say our imaginations are evil?"

It is a pervasive opinion, and there are understandable reasons for it. I think it is founded on the fact that whenever the King James Version of the Bible uses the word "imagination," it does so in a negative sense (e.g., "Every imagination of the thoughts of his heart was only evil continually" [Gen 6:5]). Clearly, if we are going to speak of a "biblical imagination," we need to address this valid concern.

In the Old Testament, the King James Version uses the term "imagination" seventeen times (Gen 6:5; Deut 29:19; Prov 6:18; Jer 3:17; Lam 3:60). In four of those references, the Hebrew word "heart" (*lav*) is used. Literally, the Old Testament speaks of the "conceptions" of the heart (Gen 6:5), the stubbornness of the heart (Deut 29:19; Jer 3:17) and the evil plots of the heart (Prov 6:18). In the Old Testament, plots and evil schemes happen in the heart. There is no singular word for "imagination" in Hebrew.

In the New Testament, the word "imagination" appears three times in the King James (Lk 1:51; Rom 1:21; 2 Cor 10:5). In these references, two of the three also refer to the heart (*kardia*). In the first reference, Mary is singing. She rejoices at the radical reversal her baby boy will bring to the world, singing literally, "By his strong arm he has thoroughly scattered the arrogant intelligence of their hearts" (Lk 1:51, author's translation). In Romans 1, Paul speaks of the coming judgment of God, saying of the wicked, "Their reasonings were futile and the understandings of their hearts were darkened" (Rom 1:21, author's translation). In the final New Testament reference in which the King James uses the word "imagination," the word "heart" (*kardia*) does not appear, but it is safe to say it is implied.

In the New Testament as in the Old, the heart is a place of dark reasonings. The problem, then, is not in the word "imagination." The problem is in the heart. The Word of God seeks to recapture and redeem our hearts for God's glory. Is the heart wicked? Without a doubt, yes! Should our hearts be involved in understanding the Bible? Without a doubt, yes!

Back to the original question. When we imagine, what are we actually doing? I don't pretend to fully understand the mystery of the human heart, but I believe that when we imagine, something is taking place in our hearts. Our minds are working with our hearts to create images (hence *image*-nation). But the heart and mind must work in concert; they must be connected by a bridge. This bridge is the imagination. It connects the heart and mind. It seeks to reintegrate and reconnect after the fragmentation brought about by the Fall. An imagination that has been surrendered to God for this process of listening to the Scriptures is what I call the "biblical imagination."

(Before we move on to the next point, you might want to put this book down and think about what's been said thus far. Take time to turn it over in your own heart, to go back to the biblical references above to confirm this notion of the surrendered heart and the biblical imagination.)

Finally, let's discuss what the word "informed" means. In this Biblical Imagination Series we speak of "engaging with Scripture at the level of the informed imagination." This was the approach of my friend and mentor, the late William Lane. It is an approach that shaped everything he did, from the writing of two major commentaries to how he lived out his daily extraordinary life. An informed imagination is willing to do the homework, refer to the commentaries. Because, unlike God, we must create from something.

I opened above with a cozy account of Jesus calling his disciples from Mark 1:17. I began by painting the scene—that is, by imagining it as you and I have probably done many times before. It is an attractive picture, but not necessarily a biblical one. You see, it was imagined by an uninformed imagination. Let's retell the same scene from a more biblically informed perspective.

Jesus has recently returned from his ordeal in the wilderness where, as only Mark tells us, he was "with the wild beasts." Perhaps in his countenance there is still some reflection of this intense period of temptation. Also, he has just discovered that his cousin John has been thrown into prison by the bloodthirsty Herod Antipas. It doesn't require Jesus' prophetic imagination to know that John's life will not last much longer. We will see in Mark an ever-present shadow of the prospect of persecution. That shadow looms large over this opening scene. It is not cozy. It is ominous.

Finally, there is the business of Jesus' creative appeal to the tired fisherman, that he will make them "fishers of men." Once we spend some time with the Jesus of the Gospels, we quickly learn that almost everything he says is rooted in the Old Testament. He breathes the

Torah. This opening appeal is no different.

Jesus' statement refers to the book of Jeremiah, the weeping prophet. (I have sometimes wondered if people mistook Jesus for Jeremiah because he was so open with his tears; see Matthew 16:14.) The passage in Jeremiah is the prelude to a song about the day of disaster. God says, "But now I will send for many fishermen . . . and they will catch them" (Jer 16:16 NIV).

This passage is about judgment and destruction. This is the background to Jesus' words in the first chapter of Mark. It is not a cozy scene but one shadowed by the serious nature of the mission to which the disciples will soon be called. Jesus' words are neither warm nor inviting. They are ominous and powerful. The task of fishing for men and women is deadly serious business. Once we have done our homework, we return to the passage with an informed imagination. Only then does it come to life. (Even the image of the sand between the disciples' toes is wrong. The shore of Galilee is extremely rocky. Neither would it have been a silent moment. Galilee is the major flyway between Africa and Europe. The sound of birds is always present!)

I agree with those who would be cautious of using the word "imagination," for with an uninformed imagination, Jesus is merely a figment. But when the imagination is surrendered along with the heart and mind, it becomes a unifying bridge that opens the Scriptures in new and exciting ways.

This volume is the second in a series that intends to overview all four Gospels. It is an attempt to model this approach of "engaging with the Scriptures at the level of the informed imagination." It is not an academic commentary, although I make use of the best academic commentaries. Neither is it a devotional commentary, though I hope it leads to a deeper devotion in those who read it. I intend to take seriously the author of each of the Gospels insofar as their individual backgrounds shape the text. We will compare what is unique about each account, always mindful of the flow of Jesus' ministry. I also hope to present relevant historical backgrounds where they are illuminating. Most of all, I hope these books will be seen as an invitation to an ongoing conversation, hopefully to many conversations.

Jesus, I struggle sometimes thinking that you are somehow a figment of my imagination, that somehow I have dreamed you up from bits and pieces of the Bible. But I want to know you in reality, Lord. I ask—we ask—that you give us the discipline to listen to your Word with all of our hearts and all of our minds. That you would renew and reveal your true self from your Word and shatter our many illusions. Give us eyes to see, make our hearts resonate—not with a figment of our imaginations but with a real person revealed in our hearts and minds. Amen.

Introduction

WHO IS MARK?

*I*t was the third time Peter had been in prison. Before, he had only been held for questioning. This final imprisonment would have ended in his death—except that an angel intervened. The angel prodded the sleeping Peter, who was not quite awake as he wandered out of the prison, past the guards and through the iron gate that eerily opened all by itself. Peter thought it was a dream until the angel disappeared and he was left dangerously exposed in the middle of the street. What to do now? Where should he go?

He ran to the only place he could think of, pounding on the outer door, pleading to be let in. The slave girl Rhoda recognized his familiar voice. He was well known to the entire household; perhaps he had first come with Jesus and experienced their last supper together. The fledgling church met in this house for prayer. In fact, they had been praying for Peter that very night even as the luminous angel was answering their prayers. The owner of the large two-story house within the walls of Jerusalem was named Mary. In Acts 12, we hear the name of her son for the very first time: John Mark. He was an extraordinary young man.

The name Marcus means "hammer"; it is a good Roman name. He is mentioned only eight times in the New Testament (see appendix D), but these references tell us all we need to know about him and more. His home might be considered the first church. How appropriate that he should write the very first story of the life of Jesus, the very first Gospel, a completely new literary form.

Mark was a cousin of Barnabas, one of the first missionaries and a leader in the early church. It has been said of Barnabas that he believed in the work God was doing in a person's life. He was the first person to recognize that Paul's conversion had been genuine (Acts 9:27). He surely believed in young John Mark, who traveled with him and Paul on their famine relief mission (Acts 11:27-30; 12:25) as well as on their first missionary journey (Acts 13:5). In Acts 13:13, for reasons we will never know, Mark called it quits and left the two leaders on the mission field in Perga, just before they would have headed into the mountainous interior (Acts 15:37, 39). Barnabas stood by his young cousin when no one else did. When he and Paul were setting out on the second missionary journey, he stood with Mark against Paul's judgment (Acts 15:36-41). Later, Mark regained Paul's trust and became a close partner in his work toward the end of his life (Philem 24; 2 Tim 4:11).

Present at the birth of the church in his own home, cousin to Barnabas, fellow worker with Paul, above all Mark is known for his relationship with Peter. The earliest church fathers agree with one voice that Mark wrote his Gospel while he was a companion of Peter, that Mark's Gospel is in a sense the memoir of Peter—Peter's spiritual remembrances (see appendix A).

As Luke remained with Paul till the bitter end (2 Tim 4:11), so it is believed that Mark stayed faithfully by Peter's side until his death. In one of his final letters Peter says as much, referring to Mark tenderly as "my son" (1 Pet 5:13). In his final letter Peter promises he will "make every effort that after my departure [read: death] you may be able to recall these things at any time" (2 Pet 1:15). I imagine him looking up from the parchment as he writes these words, perhaps smiling across the room at his "son" Mark, who might have already begun writing his Gospel.

Mark is the shortest Gospel but not necessarily because of any lack of detail. In fact, when Matthew borrows from Mark he always shortens the stories to make room for his theological agenda of portraying Jesus as the fulfillment of the Torah. Mark has no agenda besides telling the story of Jesus. He is simply recording what Peter remembers. And the simplicity of his story is an invitation to savor each and every detail.

Peter's fingerprints are all over Mark's Gospel. Only Mark tells us that the Sabbath was made for man (Mk 2:27) and that Jesus declared all foods clean (Mk 7:19). These details would have loomed large in the memory of the man who was told to "kill and eat" (Acts 10:13). The numerous references to Jesus' emotions have come down to us from his highly emotional best friend Peter. Only Mark tells us that Jesus' family thought he was "out of his mind" (Mk 3:21)—a detail only an intimate friend would have shared.

Above all, only Mark gives us the literal voice of Jesus. Again and again he records Jesus speaking in his own native Aramaic tongue (Mk 5:41; 7:11, 34; 14:36). It is as if Peter could still hear Jesus speaking as he recounted the stories to Mark. If we want to hear the literal voice of Jesus, we must learn to listen to Mark.

Mark, responding to the needs of his community, records Peter's memories of Jesus. There is an urgency; Peter is armed by Jesus with the knowledge of his own death and sees his life coming to a close. Mark is not a self-conscious writer like Luke, who spoke of the details of his own task (Lk 1:1-4). Mark simply acts as a mirror for his spiritual father. His brevity demands our attention. In his Gospel, everything matters. Perhaps without knowing it, he is teaching us how to listen to the very voice of Jesus. Selflessly, he never mentions his impressive credentials; in fact he never even mentions his own name. When we listen to his Gospel, we place ourselves at the feet of Jesus' closest earthly companion.

MAJOR THEMES

THE SO-CALLED MESSIANIC SECRET

The "messianic secret," an idea championed by William Wrede in the
1960s, was considered a major theme in Mark's Gospel for years, but
recently it has lost favor. For one thing, this theme is not exclusive to
Mark. Matthew gives us four examples (Mt 8:3-4; 9:29-31; 12:15; 17:9).
Luke provides three (Lk 4:41; 8:56; 9:21).

While it is true (and also fascinating) that Jesus occasionally charged
people to keep secret either something he had done or his identity as
the Messiah, Wrede was wrong to propose that this theme was Mark's
literary invention. Of the twenty-one miracles in Mark's Gospel, only
six involve a command for secrecy from Jesus. On at least one occasion
Jesus orders a person he has healed to go and spread the news (Mk 5:1-
19). Though Jesus is sometimes guarded about revealing his true identity, clearly he did not come to make a secret of it. So what is really
going on?

The first occurrence of Jesus' request for secrecy helps explain many
of those that follow. In Mark 1:40 Jesus has just healed a leper. In verses
43 and 44 he sternly warns the man, "See that you say nothing to anyone." But how could anyone be expected to keep something so wonderful a secret? Instead, says Mark, the healed man "went out and began
to proclaim it widely and to spread the news, with the result that Jesus
could no longer enter a town openly. But He was out in deserted places"
(Mk 1:45).

Jesus understands the nature of human beings, that they would easily become hyperfocused on his giftedness. Which is precisely what happens. As a result of the man's inability to keep quiet, Jesus' real ministry of preaching the good news is severely hampered. Does he want to keep his Messiahship a secret? No, but he intends to be selective about whom he will reveal himself to until the work of his Father is completed.

This selectivity is most clearly evident in one of the last occurrences of the so-called messianic secret. In Mark 8 Peter makes his great confession: "You are the Messiah!" (v. 29). It is a watershed moment in their time together. At last the question "Who is this man?" has been conclusively answered. But the words have scarcely left Peter's lips when Jesus warns his disciples "to tell no one about Him" (Mk 8:30). Immediately in the following verses Jesus begins to explain to them what it really means to be the Christ. He has to "undeceive" them.

Jesus commands his disciples to be silent about his identity as Messiah because they are only gradually learning what the term means. But he does reveal it to them, deliberately and selectively. Jesus instructs those he has healed to be silent in order to prevent the ever-growing mob from inundating his ministry. When he encounters people who are forced to confess his divine character because of demon possession, he commands them to be silent as well; he does not want his identity heard from the lips of demoniacs.

THE FIERY TRIAL

"Loved ones, do not think it is strange, the fiery ordeal you are suffering."
1 PETER 4:12 (AUTHOR'S TRANSLATION)

In the hot early-morning hours of July 19 in A.D. 64, the city of Rome was preparing to celebrate a religious festival dedicated to Caesar. The climax of the festival would be a series of chariot races at the Circus Maximus, an arena featuring the largest wooden structure ever built. It was perched atop massive arcades of stone and could comfortably seat more than two hundred thousand people. Later it would be expanded to hold three hundred thousand.

From the northeast corner of the stadium, a column of smoke began to slowly rise from underneath the wooden superstructure. Fanned by an unusually strong wind, the fire quickly spread, engulfing the entire arena and quickly spreading to the surrounding tumbledown houses. At first the police tried to battle the blaze with buckets of water, but they soon gave up.

The first day the fire spread throughout the flat portion of the city. On the second day the wind shifted, driving the flames up into the hills. For five days the fire burned out of control until it reached the surrounding fields and firebreaks—buildings knocked down by Roman soldiers to hem in the fire. Later that day the fire mysteriously broke out again and spread into previously untouched areas of the city. The second fire seemed to have been deliberately set on the property of Tigellinus, the captain of the Praetorian Guard. People became suspicious.

The fire burned for two more days until finally it was exhausted. Of the fourteen regions of the city of Rome, three were laid flat by the flames and seven more were virtually destroyed. Only four were untouched. The flames had been so hot they melted the marble of the temples. Scientists have since determined that the temperature of the firestorm reached eleven hundred degrees Fahrenheit.

In the refugee camps surrounding the city, stories began to circulate about mysterious groups of men who were seen moving through the city, tossing lit torches into open doorways. When townspeople tried to stop them they replied, "We are under orders to allow the flames to spread."

The suspicions of the public quickly focused on Nero. In the days following the fire he did his best to appear benevolent and supportive, lowering the price of grain and volunteering to clear the rubble at the city's expense, but he was not able to shift the blame away from himself. Roman historians Tacitus, Suetonius and Cassius Dio all determined that Nero had ordered the city burned to make room for a personal building project. Though the tradition that he fiddled while Rome burned cannot be true (the fiddle had not yet been invented!), it is true that he was in Antium, his hometown, singing a song about the destruction of Troy when the fire broke out. Two days later, when he finally sailed back to his burning city, people overheard him commenting on the beauty of the flames. (Tacitus and Suetonius have the most to say about Nero's involvement in the great fire of Rome. See appendix C.)

It is this fire and subsequent persecution that Peter refers to in his first letter (1 Pet 4:12). If we read the first half of the book closely, suffering seems a real but remote possibility. This first section closes with an "amen" (1 Pet 4:11), possibly marking the letter's original ending. Then something horrendous appears to have happened. Peter picks up his pen once more. By the time he writes the second half of his letter, he is forced to use a code word for Rome: Babylon (1 Pet 5:13). For the rest of the letter it is almost as if Peter is whispering. The persecution reported by Tacitus has become a reality for the flock Jesus entrusted to Peter. During this time Mark, Peter's "son," is with him (1 Pet 5:13), perhaps already writing his Gospel, a book William Lane referred to as a "pamphlet for hard times." Both Paul and Peter will eventually die in the first wave of persecution after the fire.

THE GOSPEL OF PASSION:
THE EMOTIONAL LIFE OF JESUS

How do I make sure Jesus isn't just a figment of my imagination, a puzzle of pieces made up out of my southern white Christian American background? If that imaginary Jesus were to come face to face with the Nazarene of the Gospels, who would win? How would I know the right one won?

Mark's Gospel offers a perfect solution. More than any other Gospel it presents the emotional life of Jesus, lifted from the imagination of Peter, himself no stranger to the emotional. The Jesus of Mark seldom resembles the "gentle Jesus, meek and mild" I grew up loving and wanting to follow. Of course we do find the compassionate Christ in Mark (Mk 1:41; 6:34; 8:2), but often we encounter the unfamiliar angry, irritated, impatient and indignant Jesus. Mark's picture of Jesus is more human than the theologically correct "fully human" Jesus in my mind.

In Mark 9:19, exasperated, Jesus asks the dim disciples, "How long must I put up with you?" A dozen commentaries explain away this moment, putting Jesus back in his safe, traditional place. Mark will have none of it, and we are left standing alone before an emotional Jesus, afraid he might say the same thing to us. When Peter is rebuked (Mk 8:33), Mark means for you and me to feel Jesus' disdain as well.

A revealing way to analyze and compare the emotional portrayals of Jesus in the Gospels is to simply count adjectives, to look at the "adjectival evidence" (see appendix B):

- Matthew uses only four adjectives in six scenes to describe the emotions of Jesus.

- Luke provides one more, making a total of seven scenes that utilize an adjective to describe Jesus' emotions. But Luke does not shy away from portraying the emotions of everyone around Jesus. In a staggering thirty-four separate scenes he uses a number of adjectives to describe the emotions of everyone from Mary to Peter to the Pharisees.

- John presents the least emotional Jesus, with only four adjectival references.

- Mark presents fifteen separate scenes that utilize a number of adjectives to paint the most varied image of the emotional life of Jesus. Mysteriously, after Mark 14:34, the adjectives disappear and Jesus seems almost emotionless.

In Mark's Gospel we should be prepared to meet a Jesus who shocks us and fails to meet our expectations. This was the experience of everyone who came close to him. Even as I write these words I have a deep appreciation for Mark's trust and willingness to present the unveiled emotional life of Jesus.

One note: In order to contrast and compare the four Gospels, it is necessary to speak in terms of Mark's Jesus or Luke's Jesus. Certainly they are one and the same person. The different perspectives of the Gospel writers provide a four-dimensional image of this infinitely complex and yet profoundly simple man.

MARK 1

THE GOOD NEWS OF JESUS—
CHRIST AND GOD'S SON

1:1 Title and outline.

THE OVERWHELMING SIGNIFICANCE OF JOHN

1:2-8 The ministry of John the Baptist.

IN THE WILDERNESS

1:9-13 The baptism and temptation of the Son.

HIS FIRST WORDS

1:14-15 Jesus' message.

1:16-20 His first disciples.

INITIAL UNHINDERED SUCCESS

1:21-28 The beginning of the ministry.

WHY HE HAS COME

1:29-39 His purpose to preach.

AN EMOTIONAL WINDOW

1:40-45 A look at his complex emotions.

THE GOOD NEWS OF JESUS—
CHRIST AND GOD'S SON

¹The beginning of the gospel of Jesus Christ, the Son of God.

*W*hen we listen to the text of Scripture with our heart and mind fully engaged, we should almost hear the tone of the author's voice. When I listen to the opening verse of Mark, I hear an enthusiastic young man who is almost out of breath.

He is speaking to us from the midst of a crisis in Rome, which is reason enough for the sense of immediacy and haste that permeates his Gospel. He is recording for us the living memories of Simon Peter, known to be exceedingly emotional himself. As we strive to listen together to Mark's voice, to his concentrated telling of the miracle that is Jesus of Nazareth, we will constantly be reminded of his urgency by his frequent use of the historical present tense (over a hundred and fifty instances), by his repeated use of the word "immediately" (*eutheos*) and by his frenetic use of "and" (*kai*) to string together his ideas.

His literary voice is simple and urgent. He has no time for personal or theological agendas, no inclination toward prosaic language. From the outset, let's tune our ears to the earnest urgency of Mark.

Some have wondered if Mark intended verse 1 to be a title for the book. He would have known that the phrase "the beginning" would remind his few Jewish readers in Rome of Genesis 1:1, "In the beginning . . . ," and the opening of the Old Testament. As the first words of Genesis spoke of the promise of a new beginning, a new creation, so Mark begins his Gospel with the same hope. His story is about everything made new.

In referring to the story of Jesus as a "gospel," Mark would have caught the attention of his Roman listeners. The word "gospel" or "evangel" was a thoroughly Roman term connected to pagan festivals and the cult of the emperor. It means "good news." An inscription celebrating the birth of Octavian reads, "The birthday of the god was for the world the beginning of 'joyful tidings.'"[1] Mark's first hearers would have immediately understood that he was referring to good news that was a cause for celebration, a historical event that would introduce a radically new situation to the world.

The use of the word "gospel" in association with the life of Jesus was nothing new. Paul, whom Mark had accompanied on his first missionary journey, used the word more than eighty times in his letters. Yet the word is being reborn in Mark's Gospel. He is the only evangelist to refer to his work by that term. Though Matthew and Luke both use "gospel" in the body of their writings, never do they refer to their books as such. In fact, Paul, Matthew and Luke always use the phrase "the gospel." Mark is the first person to present "a Gospel." In verse 1 we are witnessing the birth of a new literary form, the telling of the story of a life, which is at the same time a testimony. It is one of the most extraordinary sentences in the New Testament.

More than a title, verse 1 also presents Mark's broad outline. His account is simple and straightforward, comprising only two parts. Both sections establish the twofold identity of Jesus as Christ and God's Son.

The first section, from Mark 1:1 to 8:30, presents Jesus as the Messiah, the Christ. With Jesus' baptism, Mark begins to tell the story of the first disciples and Jesus' early ministry. A common thread throughout is the disciples' confusion over who Jesus is. It comes to a finale when Peter confesses Jesus as the Messiah. Being the faithful Jew he was, Mark lived in the hope and expectation of the appearance of the Messiah. He would have heard such rabbinic teachings as "He who, when he prays, does not pray for the coming of the Messiah, has not prayed at all." The appearing of Jesus promised to fulfill his spiritual, political and economic hopes. It would be the solution to every problem, the answer to every question. At least that is what Mark and his contemporaries believed.

The second section begins with Mark 8:31 and comes to a dramatic conclusion with the confession of the centurion at the crucifixion, who declared in Mark 15:39, "Truly this man was the Son of God" (ASV). In the course of Mark's narrative, we will gradually discover that Jesus is truly the Messiah and uniquely the Son of God. Mark takes us on a long, disturbing journey. If we listen with fully engaged imaginations, we will find ourselves at the end of his Gospel with the women outside the empty tomb. There we will be forced to make our own personal decision about who Jesus truly is.

THE OVERWHELMING SIGNIFICANCE OF JOHN

²As it is written in Isaiah the prophet:

Look, I am sending My messenger ahead of You,
who will prepare Your way.
³A voice of one crying out in the wilderness:
"Prepare the way for the Lord;
make His paths straight!"

⁴John came baptizing in the wilderness and preaching a baptism of repentance for the forgiveness of sins. ⁵The whole Judean countryside and all the people of Jerusalem were flocking to him, and they were baptized by him in the Jordan River as they confessed their sins. ⁶John wore a camel-hair garment with a leather belt around his waist and ate locusts and wild honey. ⁷He was preaching: "Someone more powerful than I will come after me. I am not worthy to stoop down and untie the strap of His sandals. ⁸I have baptized you with water, but He will baptize you with the Holy Spirit."

The first voice we hear in Mark's Gospel is not Jesus' voice but Malachi's. Mark quotes the prophet's veiled prediction of the ministry of John the Baptist, a promise found in the closing words of Malachi (Mal 3:1; 4:5-6). In a single breath, we have both the final promise of God in the Old Testament and its fulfillment in the opening of the New.

When we meet him in Mark, John is standing in the Jordan with his camel-hair coat, preaching repentance. Repentance—it is the only way the people would be prepared to meet the one who was coming to forgive their sins. That is how John "prepares the way" for Jesus. In the course of the story we will meet men and women who have come to Jesus with repentant hearts because they had, no doubt, heard the preaching of John.

The prophetic voice abruptly shifts. Now it is Isaiah's voice we hear in the wilderness. It is crying out in the Baptist's hoarse words that the path, which was crooked, will be made straight. It will no longer be a meandering passage that twists and turns; from now on the way will lead straight to Jesus, the Messiah.

John is all that is old and everything that is new. He stands with one foot in the Old Testament and the other firmly planted in the New. It is impossible to overstate his significance. He was so famous in his time that he merited mention in the writings of Josephus (see appendix C). In every Gospel the story of Jesus' ministry begins with that of John. When Peter and Paul present their accounts of the life of Jesus, they will begin with John as well (Acts 1:22; 10:37; 13:24-25). The prophetic voice of God, silent for four hundred years, has begun to speak once more in him. He will become the focus of Herod Antipas. Mark, so known for his brevity, will give a peculiarly lengthy account of John's death (Mk 6:14-29).

John is the "Elijah who is to come" (Mt 11:14). From the wilderness, clothed in camel hair, eating locusts and honey and screaming Elijah's message (2 Kings 1:8; Mk 9:9-13), he enters the scene with a tremendous following, attracting the attention of a king. Years later Paul will still encounter John's disciples in far-off Ephesus (Acts 19:4). Each of the Gospels provides its own unique tribute to John. Matthew's is the lengthiest (Mt 11:7-19). In it Jesus praises his cousin, saying, "Among those born of women no one greater than John the Baptist has appeared" (Mt 11:11). Luke honors John by telling of his miraculous birth in parallel with Jesus' (Lk 1:5-80). In the Gospel of John, in a lengthy passage concerning the prophet (Jn 5:31-38), Jesus proclaims that he was a "burning and shining lamp" (v. 35).

The object of prophecy, the product of a miraculous birth, the focus of both the great and lowly, John has every reason to be prideful. But such is not the case. His message, says Mark in 1:7, is clothed with radical humility. Jesus is more powerful, John preaches. While he merely baptizes with water, Jesus will immerse his followers in the Holy Spirit. (Mark omits "and fire"—see Matthew 3:11—in light of the situation; his readers were suffering in the wake of the conflagration that destroyed Rome.) The task of loosening the sandals was performed by the lowliest of slaves, but John is not worthy to do even that for Jesus.

Yet Jesus will exceed John even in his humility. Jesus will go beyond the lowly task of loosening the sandal. He will wash his disciples' feet (Jn 13:5-17).

IN THE WILDERNESS

⁹In those days Jesus came from Nazareth in Galilee and was baptized in the Jordan by John. ¹⁰As soon as He came up out of the water, He saw the heavens being torn open and the Spirit descending to Him like a dove. ¹¹And a voice came from heaven:

> *You are My beloved Son;*
> *I take delight in You!*

¹²Immediately the Spirit drove Him into the wilderness. ¹³He was in the wilderness 40 days, being tempted by Satan. He was with the wild animals, and the angels began to serve Him.

*T*he journey from Nazareth to the Jordan River, where tradition says Jesus was baptized, would have taken ten days to two weeks on foot. As Jesus made his lonely way south along the shaded path that lay beside the river, he could at any moment have turned back from all that was awaiting him and returned to the safety of home. He had had a lifetime to ponder his decision, and for these final solitary ten days it would have loomed large in his heart and mind.

All at once, with Markan abruptness, Jesus has arrived. There is no mention of John's confusion at being asked to baptize his cousin (see Mt 3:13). In a flash it is done. Jesus has submitted to a baptism of repentance though he has nothing of which to repent. The deep desire of his heart is to embrace those of us who need to repent. His baptism speaks of his choice of solidarity with us.

We find Mark's favorite word for the first time in Mark 1:10: *eutheos*, often translated "immediately." He will use it eleven times in this chapter alone. It is the verbal razor blade he uses for the quick cuts of his fast-paced portrayal of Jesus' life. "Immediately" Jesus comes out of the water and sees a vision. He has traveled far, both physically and emotionally, to come to this place. He is exhausted and needy. The vision and the voice will provide all that he needs and more.

Heaven opens and the Spirit John just referred to descends "like a dove" (Mk 1:10). Mark refers to the Spirit only five times in his Gospel, and three of those references are here. (The remaining two are in chapters 12 and 13.) The baptism of Jesus is the only place in the Bible where the image of a dove describes the Holy Spirit. We must decide for ourselves what "like" means. Does it literally mean that a white bird landed on Jesus' shoulder? Or does it mean that the Spirit somehow fluttered, as with wings, and came to rest on him? (Acts 2 describes the Spirit as a flickering flame.) In Mark 1:11, the voice of God completes the appearance of the Trinity: the voice of the Father, the presence of the Holy Spirit, and Jesus, the Son.

The Father's first words, "You are my Son," are from Psalm 2:7. "I take delight in you" is a paraphrase from Isaiah 42:1, which begins a passage directed at the suffering servant of chapters 42 through 55. In Isaiah these are ominous words, spoken to one who would suffer for our sin and God's sake. But at the same time they are the words every son and daughter longs to hear from their father. Above all others, these are the words Jesus needs to hear from his Father at the outset of his ministry. (If you have never heard these words from your earthly father, hear them now, spoken by your heavenly Father.)

Baptism and wilderness—they are connected. One prepares us for the other. To be set apart by baptism means that a wilderness lies ahead of us. The Spirit that has descended now drives. In the original, Mark 1:12 opens with "And immediately," a double dose of Markan literary haste. Jesus is literally "thrown" or "cast" by the Spirit into the wilderness.

Without providing a single detail of the threefold temptation of Jesus, Mark characteristically abbreviates the story. Instead he adds a meaningful detail found in none of the other Gospels. Jesus, he says, was "with the wild animals." For Mark's first readers, wild animals would have been waiting in their own personal wilderness as well. With the persecution under Nero after the fire in Rome, the prospect of being thrown to the wild beasts in the arena became very real (see appendix C). Their baptism and experience of wilderness were as intertwined as was Jesus' experience.

John cries out in the desert. He comes baptizing in the desert. Jesus is driven to and tempted in the desert. Again and again in Mark's Gospel, Jesus will return to the desert. In Mark 1:35 he will retreat there to pray in solitude. In verse 45 he will be forced there by the crush of the crowds. In chapter 6 he will invite the disciples there to rest. And there, though he himself will be exhausted from ministry, he will feed five thousand.

HIS FIRST WORDS

14 After John was arrested, Jesus went to Galilee, preaching the good news of God: 15 "The time is fulfilled, and the kingdom of God has come near. Repent and believe in the good news!"

16 As He was passing along by the Sea of Galilee, He saw Simon and Andrew, Simon's brother. They were casting a net into the sea, since they were fishermen.

17 "Follow Me," Jesus told them, "and I will make you fish for people!" 18 Immediately they left their nets and followed Him. 19 Going on a little farther, He saw James the son of Zebedee and his brother John. They were in their boat mending their nets. 20 Immediately He called them, and they left their father Zebedee in the boat with the hired men and followed Him.

Though no explanation is given, it appears that Jesus' ministry did not, perhaps could not, begin until John's had ended (see Lk 4:14). The fundamental message they shared—"repent"—appears identical. But their ministries could not have been more different. John baptized with water, Jesus with the Holy Spirit. Obedience to John's message involved waiting for the Messiah. Obedience to Jesus' message meant following him.

If we are to accompany Jesus around Galilee in our imaginations, we need an accurate picture of the countryside. The province of Galilee is roughly fifty miles long by twenty-five miles wide. On its eastern border is the freshwater Lake of Galilee, about fourteen miles long and

seven miles wide. Wherever you stand you can see the entire sweep of
the lake. This explains how the crowds could follow Jesus around the
shore while he crossed the lake in a boat. Standing on the shore of that
lake, which is surrounded by modest hills, you get the distinct impres-
sion that this is the only world that exists. I think of Galilee as a self-
contained world.

In Jesus' day Galilee was the most densely populated province in the
Middle East.[2] Josephus, who had once been governor, estimated the
population at fifteen thousand. This helps us understand how a massive
mob could come together to follow Jesus and why it was sometimes difficult for him to get away from the crowd. Galilee was a strategic area
to plant the ministry.

Mark 1:15 reads, "The time is fulfilled, and the kingdom of God has
come near. Repent and believe the good news!" A more literal translation of "believe the good news" would be "trust in the gospel." The
kingdom, the reign of God, has come near because God's son is here
among us. To follow him one must turn around and move in a totally
different direction, away from the things of the world and toward him.
It is good news. It is the best news!

Jesus began preaching before he chose the Twelve. The ministry
started without them. They were privileged to be invited to become a
part of it, as are we. Perhaps because Peter was Mark's source, Peter is
the first disciple we meet. He and his brother Andrew are on the shore
casting their nets into the shallows. The word used here for "casting" is
a *hapax legomenon*, a word that only occurs once in the Bible. Perhaps
the uniqueness of the language indicates that Peter, a fisherman who
speaks in technical language, is our eyewitness.

The Gospel of John tells us that Jesus and Peter have already met (Jn
1:40-42). Andrew had been a follower of John the Baptist and had
brought his brother to meet Jesus earlier. This is not the first time
they've laid eyes on each other.

"Come follow me" (Mk 1:17) is not an offer nor an invitation. It is a
command to be met either with obedience or disobedience. It is a call
they can respond to or ignore. Andrew and Peter, in Markan style, respond "immediately." The phrase "fishers of men" (Mk 1:17 NIV) comes

to us from the Old Testament. It is not a clever pitch but a sobering call to become part of the serious business of the gospel. In Jeremiah 16:16, these words speak of judgment. But that image will shift as Jesus takes on himself the judgment of the world. The men and women who are "caught" by the disciples will be spared the judgment precisely because Jesus will give himself in their place. The net cast by the Twelve will save the fish, not lead to their destruction.

Farther down the rocky shore, the three encounter three more, a father and his two sons. Unlike Peter and Andrew, James and John are in a boat putting their nets in order. They have been deep-draft fishing rather than casting nets into the shallows as Peter and Andrew were doing. James and John's response is also "immediate." Hearing the call, they leave their father and his hired servants. It is the last time we will see Zebedee in the Gospels. I often wonder if it was the last time James and John saw him as well.

"The time has come" are Jesus' first words in the Gospel of Mark (Mk 1:15). In any well-told story, the opening words of the central character set the tone and direction for the rest of the narrative. And when Jesus announces that the "time" has come, Mark uses the Greek word *kairos*, which refers to the supreme moment, as opposed to *chronos*, or sequential time. This is the ultimate kairotic moment. Jesus has come and issued his call, his command. If you and I are engaged in listening to the Gospel of Mark, we will take our places beside Peter, Andrew, James and John and decide, in the framework of this supreme moment, how we will respond.

INITIAL UNHINDERED SUCCESS

²¹Then they went into Capernaum, and right away He entered the synagogue on the Sabbath and began to teach. ²²They were astonished at His teaching because, unlike the scribes, He was teaching them as one having authority.

²³Just then a man with an unclean spirit was in their synagogue. He cried out, ²⁴"What do You have to do with us, Jesus—Nazarene? Have You come to destroy us? I know who You are—the Holy One of God!"

²⁵But Jesus rebuked him and said, "Be quiet, and come out of him!"

²⁶And the unclean spirit convulsed him, shouted with a loud voice, and came out of him.

²⁷Then they were all amazed, so they began to argue with one another, saying, "What is this? A new teaching with authority! He commands even the unclean spirits, and they obey Him." ²⁸News about Him then spread throughout the entire vicinity of Galilee.

*T*he next scene occurs "immediately," as Jesus and the disciples enter Capernaum and the synagogue. This story will be unique; Jesus will perform a miracle on the Sabbath, in the synagogue, and yet there will be no conflict. In contrast, Luke tells us of one Sabbath when Jesus preached in the synagogue in Nazareth and was violently expelled. It appears he never returned to Nazareth (Lk 4:17-27).

Now Capernaum becomes Jesus' adopted home. There he experiences unhindered success. Though Mark omits the content of Jesus' teaching, he does record the response of the congregation. They are astonished. They have never heard anything like it. How do they describe the uniqueness of Jesus' teaching? One word: *authority*. The word Mark uses implies a supernatural authority.

It should be no surprise that what comes next is a supernatural confrontation with a demon-possessed man. Jesus' presence and authority provoke a response from the demoniac. Listen to the confusion in his pronouns. "What do You have to do with *us*? . . . *I* know who You are" (Mk 1:24, emphasis added). These supernatural forces, though they are demonic in nature, recognize Jesus' identity as the "Holy One of God" (Mk 1:24; see also Jas 2:19). But Jesus does not seem to want this confession to be heard from the voice of a demon.

This is our first glimpse into the emotional life of Jesus. The Greek word Mark uses for "rebuked" implies a threat (Mk 1:25); sometimes it is translated "sternly rebuked." Literally, Jesus commands the demon to "be muzzled" (it is the same command he will give the storm in chapter 4). The response is immediate. The man convulses and is set free.

The Roman-Jewish historian Josephus gives an account of a very different sort of exorcism, which he personally witnessed. A traveling exorcist named Eleazar performed a demonstration for Vespasian (who would eventually become emperor) and his men. His method, which was common practice, was to place a ring of secret herbs under the nose of the possessed person. The herbs would force a sneeze, whereby the demon supposedly left through the nostrils. At that moment Eleazar would command the demon, in the name of Solomon, never to return.[3]

When we compare Josephus' story with Mark's account we understand why the Caperneans recognized something new in Jesus. He required no herbs, no incantations, no appeal to the power of the name of someone like Solomon. Jesus simply issued a command, which the demons had no choice but to obey.

WHY HE HAS COME

[29]*As soon as they left the synagogue, they went into Simon and Andrew's house with James and John.* [30]*Simon's mother-in-law was lying in bed with a fever, and they told Him about her at once.* [31]*So He went to her, took her by the hand, and raised her up. The fever left her, and she began to serve them.*

[32]*When evening came, after the sun had set, they began bringing to Him all those who were sick and those who were demon-possessed.* [33]*The whole town was assembled at the door,* [34]*and He healed many who were sick with various diseases and drove out many demons. But He would not permit the demons to speak, because they knew Him.*

[35]*Very early in the morning, while it was still dark, He got up, went out, and made His way to a deserted place. And He was praying there.* [36]*Simon and his companions went searching for Him.* [37]*They found Him and said, "Everyone's looking for You!"*

[38]*And He said to them, "Let's go on to the neighboring villages so that I may preach there too. This is why I have come."* [39]*So He went into all of Galilee, preaching in their synagogues and driving out demons.*

*P*eter's house is a short eighty-three-foot walk down a narrow alley from the synagogue. Andrew is there and so is Peter's mother-in-law. Ordinarily, upon the death of her husband, she would have lived with her own immediate family, probably one of her sons. Though we do not know why she is living with Peter and his wife, it hints at Peter's generous character that she is there. Strictly speaking she is not his responsibility. Yet there she is being provided for. The Gospels imply that Jesus made Peter's house his home. It would have been a crowded place, though Jesus never stayed put for very long.

Mark tells us that Jesus and the disciples came "immediately" to the house, only to find the mother-in-law ill. Luke, the doctor, tells us she had a "high fever" (Lk 4:38), which in the first century would have been serious. It might be too much to say that she was dying, but if her condition did not change, she would move headlong toward the grave.

Mark says Jesus simply took her by the hand and raised her up (Mk 1:31). Luke tells us he "rebuked" the fever (Lk 4:39). It is another example of the supernatural authority we saw in the synagogue a few minutes ago, just eighty-three feet up the dark alleyway.

It is natural for Jesus to reach out to this woman in healing compassion. Likewise, it is natural for her to rise and set about serving the guests. We know nothing about this privileged woman, and less than nothing about her daughter, who would give up everything for the gospel and travel with her husband (1 Cor 9:5). We do have a portrait by Peter of his ideal woman in 1 Peter 3:1-6. She is pure and reverent. Her unadorned beauty radiates from within. Her spirit is gentle and quiet. Could this be a sketch of Peter's wife, and perhaps also of her mother?

The success of Jesus' new ministry grows. After sunset Peter's house is thronged with people who have heard the rumors and brought their sick and demon-possessed relations for healing. Listen closely to the text and you will hear not a word of Jesus' preaching or teaching. Not a single word. The crowds have come only to receive his gifts, not to hear him. Throughout Mark's Gospel, crowds will be intent on using Jesus. This explains why he is constantly moving, crisscrossing the lake in order to get away from them. He has come not to give his gifts but himself.

Earlier, in the synagogue, the demon-possessed man declared that Jesus was the "Holy One of God," and Jesus commanded him to be silent. Mark 1:34 states that this is an ongoing problem. Jesus does not want his true nature to be confessed by demons. It is the beginning of a secretive element of Jesus' ministry that Mark will keep returning to in his account. The final section of this chapter makes clear why Jesus commands secrecy.

Early in the morning he slips away unnoticed, returning to "a deserted place" (Mk 1:35), also translated as "desert" or "wilderness." (In contrast to Luke, who presents Jesus at prayer during every phase of the ministry, Mark portrays Jesus at prayer only three times: Mk 1:35; 6:46; 14:39.) Though the ministry is only a few days old, it already seems to be getting beyond Jesus' control. The popularity is troubling to him. Celebrity is in conflict with his call to preach. It will be an ongoing battle for the next three years.

In Mark 1:36 the disciples have become simply "Simon and his companions," another echo of Peter's living witness in Mark. Simon is telling the story. Early in the morning everyone is looking for Jesus to heal the sick. His central purpose, to preach the good news, is in jeopardy. They must move on, Jesus says. He is not cultivating popularity. He is fleeing it. In the clarity of that early morning solitary prayer session, Jesus and his disciples set out for the first time. The ministry has begun.

What takes Matthew and Luke four long chapters to tell Mark compresses into one. Matthew has a theological agenda: to communicate Jesus' myriad connections to the Old Testament. Luke is weaving multiple strands of story concerning the Gentile mission and the theme of Jesus' radical reversal. Mark is not encumbered by any additional purpose. His bags are packed. He travels light and fast. His only concern is to tell the unadorned and concentrated story of Jesus the Messiah, the Son of God. Through the remaining pages of his extraordinary Gospel we will be called to follow a path that is often dangerous and troubling. If we are to engage with our imaginations, from this point on we will be on the road with Jesus!

AN EMOTIONAL WINDOW

40 Then a man with a serious skin disease came to Him and, on his knees, begged Him: "If You are willing, You can make me clean."

41 Moved with compassion, Jesus reached out His hand and touched him.

"I am willing," He told him. "Be made clean." ⁴²Immediately the disease left
him, and he was healed. ⁴³Then He sternly warned him and sent him away
at once, ⁴⁴telling him, "See that you say nothing to anyone; but go and show
yourself to the priest, and offer what Moses prescribed for your cleansing, as
a testimony to them." ⁴⁵Yet he went out and began to proclaim it widely and
to spread the news, with the result that Jesus could no longer enter a town
openly. But He was out in deserted places, and they would come to Him from
everywhere.

*T*hough we usually read right past it, this final passage is filled with
disturbing emotional contradictions. It is a story that troubled even
Matthew and Luke, for they chose to omit verse 43, where the problem lies.

In Mark 1:39, Jesus and the disciples move out onto the mission field
of Galilee. In verse 40 they encounter a man with a loathsome skin
disease. Perhaps they are only just on their way out of Capernaum when
they hear the sound of the warning bell around the leper's neck. He
would have been required by law to wear it and to call out to everyone
who approached him, "Unclean!"

The "if" in the leper's initial statement, "If you are willing," does not
seem to bother Jesus (in contrast, see Mk 9:23). Mark 1:41-42 describes
everything we have come to expect from Jesus. He is "moved with compassion" (literally, his guts are wrenched) by the sight and perhaps the
smell of this pitifully diseased man. But the man's life needs healing as
much as his body. Covered with festering sores, he has been cut off
from Jewish life, from community, from the synagogue, from temple
observance. Jesus defies the law when he reaches out to touch the un-
touchable man. A person who is clean touches someone who is unclean,
and for the first time in recorded history, the flow is miraculously re-
versed. It is not Jesus who becomes unclean as a result, but the unclean
man who is made whole. And it happens because of Jesus' simple, authoritative pronouncement. And as we have come to expect, it happens
"immediately."

In the next verse, Mark 1:43, everything changes. Jesus' compassionate mood seems to vanish like smoke. He is not the same person. The words "sternly warned" could just as accurately read that he was "greatly disturbed," or that he "scolded," or even that he "inveighed against" the man. And the relatively benign translation "sent him away at once" should be translated "drove him away." These are the disturbing, emotionally charged words Matthew and Luke chose to avoid. Try to imagine the tone of Jesus' voice as he tells the man—just as he earlier commanded the demons—to "say nothing to anyone" (Mk 1:44). The abrupt shift is disconcerting. This is not the Jesus of my imagination. But Mark is not interested in Jesus as a figment of the imagination. His subject is the historical Jesus, who disturbed and unsettled far more people than he comforted.

Let's attempt to understand the shift. First, Jesus is confronted by a man who falls on his knees and begs for healing. As we would expect, Jesus, the compassionate One, is deeply moved by the man's sad predicament, moved when he sees the loathsome effects of the sin-sick, death-impregnated world. He speaks the words of healing.

Next, the abrupt transition from compassion to anger. Remember that according to what Mark has already told us, Jesus' calling has been hampered by rumors of his ability to heal. They have spread like wildfire. His reputation is becoming that of a healer or "divine man," like Eleazar and the other charlatans who travel throughout Palestine. Jesus has been driven to the wilderness in an attempt to keep on task with his call to preach the good news of the kingdom, of which he is the king.

As Jesus sees the man's skin clearing, his sores beginning to vanish, the sickening smell starting to fade, he realizes what will inevitably follow: a more adamant mob, a more demanding herd of hangers-on with no interest in listening to or being transformed by his luminous words. The *best* of Jesus' call to preach the good news is being eclipsed by the *good* of his ability to heal.

This explains Jesus' abrupt emotional shift from compassion to angry frustration. Jesus is not angry with the man, who soon disobeys his request to keep silent. He is frustrated by a situation in which he feels trapped.

When the Lord called Jeremiah to his prophetic ministry, he told the weeping prophet that the people would not listen to what he had to say (Jer 7:27). Now Jesus (who will be confused with Jeremiah) finds himself in the grip of the same impossible call. This emotional moment is a small window into his deep humanity, and only Mark, with the intimate insight of Simon Peter as his source, reveals this painful facet of Jesus' life.

The final verse of the chapter, Mark 1:45, says it all. The nameless man, now healed and whole, spreads the wonderful news. Jesus saw it coming a mile away. Now he will be driven farther into the wilderness. The people, Mark tells us, begin coming from "everywhere." They are not interested in hearing the words that will nevertheless flow from Jesus' emotional heart.

Like Jeremiah, like David, like Job, Jesus flees to the wilderness where his forefathers fled. Those first forty days of testing were not the end but the beginning. The rest of his life will be lived out in one sort of wilderness or another. All who are determined to obey Jesus' command to follow must follow him there and learn for ourselves what only the wilderness can teach.

MARK 2

Stories of the Inappropriateness of Jesus

FORGIVES THE UNFORGIVABLE

2:1-12 Jesus heals the paralytic through forgiveness.

ACCEPTS THE UNACCEPTABLE

2:13-17 The calling of Levi, the tax collector.

THE OLD ORTHODOXY AND THE NEW REALITY

2:18-22 Jesus is questioned for his unorthodoxy.

LORD OVER ORTHODOXY

2:23-28 Jesus asserts his authority.

FORGIVES THE UNFORGIVABLE

[1]When He entered Capernaum again after some days, it was reported that He was at home. [2]So many people gathered together that there was no more room, not even in the doorway, and He was speaking the message to them. [3]Then they came to Him bringing a paralytic, carried by four men. [4]Since they were not able to bring him to Jesus because of the crowd, they removed the roof above where He was. And when they had broken through, they lowered the stretcher on which the paralytic was lying.

[5]Seeing their faith, Jesus told the paralytic, "Son, your sins are forgiven."

[6]But some of the scribes were sitting there, thinking to themselves: [7]"Why does He speak like this? He's blaspheming! Who can forgive sins but God alone?"

[8]Right away Jesus understood in His spirit that they were reasoning like this within themselves and said to them, "Why are you reasoning these things in your hearts? [9]Which is easier: to say to the paralytic, 'Your sins are forgiven,' or to say, 'Get up, pick up your mat, and walk'? [10]But so you may know that the Son of Man has authority on earth to forgive sins," He told the paralytic, [11]"I tell you: get up, pick up your stretcher, and go home."

[12]Immediately he got up, picked up the stretcher, and went out in front of everyone. As a result, they were all astounded and gave glory to God, saying, "We have never seen anything like this!"

*A*fter a few days, Jesus returns from his self-imposed exile back to Capernaum, his "home." Perhaps he has run out of provisions in the wilderness; Jesus will exercise his power to feed others but never himself. Predictably, the house is mobbed for the second time. Estimates for the population of Capernaum in Jesus' day range from six hundred to fifteen hundred. Even the smaller number would have clogged the narrow alleyways leading to the humble house where Jesus was staying.

For the remainder of Mark's Gospel, we must imagine Jesus constantly surrounded by a crowd of people pushing and shoving their way toward him (Mk 3:8-10, 20; 4:1; 5:21, 24, 31; 6:31, 34; 8:1; 9:14; 10:1, 46; 12:12). Twice Mark tells us that Jesus and his disciples are so mobbed they do not have a chance to eat (Mk 3:20; 8:1). In addition to attempting to avoid the crowds by moving into the wilderness, Jesus will flee all the way to Tyre and try (unsuccessfully) to keep his presence there secret (Mk 7:24).

Inside the besieged home, Jesus speaks the "message" (*logon*; Mk 1:2) to those who are able to hear above the clamor outside. Mark's Gospel can be frustrating; the author routinely omits the content of Jesus' sermons. Except for the lesson of the seed parables in chapter 4 and a long discussion of the end of the age in chapter 13, Jesus rarely speaks for more than a minute or so. If you take a red-letter edition of the Gospel of Mark and time yourself reading only Jesus' words, the total amounts to slightly more than twenty minutes. The total time to read Mark's Gospel is an hour and a half. In Luke, which requires two and a half hours to read, Jesus speaks for over an hour. Mark, who so urgently tells us the story of Jesus, pauses for only twenty precious minutes to record what Jesus actually said. His urgency is an invitation to listen intently. We have only twenty minutes of "face time" with Jesus.

As we are present at the scene in Peter's home by means of our engaged imaginations, we notice a scraping sound coming from the ceiling above Jesus' head. Soon bits of plaster and dirt are falling all around. Again, the precious lesson is interrupted. Through a jagged hole in the roof (Peter's roof!) a paralytic descends with the help of four friends. The emotional reaction we might have expected from Jesus, frustration at being interrupted yet again in the midst of his call to teach, never comes. The bizarre scene has captured Jesus' imagination! He looks up, realizing the faith required for four men to do what they have done for their paralyzed companion.

"Son" (*teknon*), Jesus says as he looks up, squinting from the sunlight, "your sins are forgiven" (Mk 2:5).

The healing is not immediate. Jesus senses what some of the scribes are thinking to themselves. (This is almost always a bad thing in the Gospels; see Lk 12:17.) Religious people believe that only God has the power to forgive sins, and then only after the sinner has engaged in rigorous acts of repentance and ritual observance. What Jesus has said is at best inappropriate. In their minds it is blasphemy.

Jesus does not confront them directly. In rabbinic fashion he responds with a question. Rabbis often formulated questions based on the phrase "how much more." It was an interpretive technique first devised by the great Jewish leader Hillel, who may have been present to hear the twelve-year-old Jesus in the temple. "So, which is easier," Jesus queries, "to say, 'Your sins are forgiven' or 'Get up and walk'?" Though commentaries disagree, it seems obvious that both are impossible. It is impossible to forgive sin unless you are God. It is equally impossible to tell a paralytic to get up and walk unless you are God.

The scribes are silent. They look on in shock as the paralytic rises from his mat and walks. Both are impossible, yet Jesus has spoken both commands: "Your sins are forgiven" in Mark 2:5 and "Get up and walk" in Mark 2:11. The visible reality of the man's healed limbs is evidence of the invisible reality that his sins have been forgiven.

It is the only occasion of Jesus healing someone by pronouncing the forgiveness of sin. In Luke 7:48 he will forgive the sins of the woman who has wept on his feet—another instance of religious leaders taking offense—but that is not a healing. This story alludes to a complicated truth that is often oversimplified. Yes, there is a connection between sickness and sin. But no, not all sin leads to physical sickness. Not all sickness is a direct result of sin. Yet it is safe to say that all sin paralyzes.

In Mark 2:10, Jesus refers to himself for the first time in this Gospel by the mysterious title "Son of Man." Fourteen times Mark's Jesus will use the designation. Like most of Jesus' language, it comes from the Old Testament, where the phrase is simply a designation for "human being." (One exception might be Daniel 7:13-14, but scholars disagree on this passage.)

In the New Testament, Jesus appropriates the title in a new way. His incarnation redefines it. One exceptional new translation renders the phrase "the human one."[4] Who but the incarnate one who has taken humanity upon himself could speak a word of forgiveness and healing and win praise for God? Who but the "human one" could enter the world so humbly yet clothed with such authority?

ACCEPTS THE UNACCEPTABLE

13 Then Jesus went out again beside the sea. The whole crowd was coming to Him, and He taught them. 14 Then, moving on, He saw Levi the son of Alphaeus sitting at the tax office, and He said to him, "Follow Me!" So he got up and followed Him.

15 While He was reclining at the table in Levi's house, many tax collectors and sinners were also guests with Jesus and His disciples, because there were many who were following Him. 16 When the scribes of the Pharisees, saw that He was eating with sinners and tax collectors, they asked His disciples, "Why does He eat with tax collectors and sinners?"

17 When Jesus heard this, He told them, "Those who are well don't need a doctor, but the sick [do need one]. I didn't come to call the righteous, but sinners."

*I*t is not clear exactly how much time elapses between Mark 2:12 and 2:13. In verse 13, the ever-present crowd is there. Jesus is teaching again, yet Mark does not give us a single word of the luminous lesson. The evidence points to the fact that Jesus is still on the outskirts of Capernaum. The other Synoptics place the call of Levi immediately after the last scene in Peter's hometown. It takes place at Levi's tax booth, which would have been located by the Via Maris, or "Way of the Sea," an ancient trade route that passed through the village.

Like Mark, Luke calls this man "Levi" when he first meets Jesus (Lk 5:27, 29); it seems to have been his given name. Only in Matthew's Gospel is he referred to at this moment as "Matthew," a nickname meaning "gift of Yahweh" (Mt 9:9). I imagine it was a name Jesus granted to him, one of which he was understandably proud. For most of his adult life Levi would probably have not seen himself as anyone's gift, certainly not God's.

Mark refers to Levi as the son of Alphaeus. In his list of the Twelve in chapter 3, he names another son of Alphaeus: James. It is possible then that the two were brothers, the sons of Alphaeus. This would mean that of the Twelve, half were brothers: Peter and Andrew, James and John, and possibly Levi and James.

Situated where he was outside of a fishing village, it is likely that Levi was collecting the "fish tax," a tariff mentioned by numerous ancient sources. In Jesus' day, tax collectors were regarded on a level with sinners. In Mark 2:15-16 they are lumped together twice! Clearly Matthew is a traitor to his people, a disgrace to his family. Most significantly, he is the last person Jesus should be adding to his ministry team. This is the second of a series of scandalous stories given to us by Mark.

The Gospels tell us of no prior acquaintance between Jesus and Levi, no previous contact. We have only Jesus' command to follow and Levi's immediate and complete response of obedience. Of all the disciples, he would have left the most behind monetarily.

In one of his characteristic quick edits, Mark cuts immediately to a banquet at Levi's home. He has invited his fellow tax collectors. It is a big party when you include the many followers Jesus would have brought along. (Levi is not the only tax collector who responded to Jesus' grace by throwing him a party. See Lk 19:6-7.)

In Mark 2:16 we meet the Pharisees for the first time in Mark's Gospel. These religious leaders were known as the "separate ones" from the Hebrew word *parush* ("to set apart"). An extreme "back to the Bible" sect, they came together sometime after the Maccabean revolt. Their piety was founded on a radical embrace of the oral law, which they believed was delivered to the elders at the same time Moses gave the written law to the priests. At a time of political and social upheaval, when many movements and sects were forming (Sadducees, Essenes, Herodians), the Pharisees had the most momentum and the widest following. Their influence has shaped the nature of Judaism into the present day.

One of the Pharisees' distinct beliefs was that the ritual cleanliness mandated by the Old Testament for the priests of Israel should be extended to all the people. It was a tremendous burden that they placed on themselves and everyone else (see Mt 23:4).

In Mark 2, these Pharisees, the "separate ones," ask Jesus' disciples why he does not separate himself from people like Levi. It is a glaringly obvious question. Very much the rabbi, Jesus responds by quoting a passage from one of their own books known as the Mekilta, an ancient commentary on the book of Exodus. "Those who are well don't need a doctor," he says, "but the sick do need one" (Mk 2:17).

I imagine Jesus placing a hand on Levi's shoulder or perhaps on another of the seedy guests at the party as he makes this irritating pronouncement. Notice that Jesus does not reject the categories of the Pharisees. He also speaks of the "righteous" and "sinners." But he makes the inappropriate choice of identifying with the sinners. In fact, he pronounces forgiveness and reaches out to them. In the eyes of the Pharisees, Jesus is oh-for-two.

THE OLD ORTHODOXY AND THE NEW REALITY

18 Now John's disciples and the Pharisees were fasting. People came and asked Him, "Why do John's disciples and the Pharisees' disciples fast, but Your disciples do not fast?"

19 Jesus said to them, "The wedding guests cannot fast while the groom is with them, can they? As long as they have the groom with them, they cannot fast. 20 But the time will come when the groom is taken away from them, and then they will fast in that day. 21 No one sews a patch of unshrunk cloth on an old garment. Otherwise, the new patch pulls away from the old cloth, and a worse tear is made. 22 And no one puts new wine into old wineskins. Otherwise, the wine will burst the skins, and the wine is lost as well as the skins. But new wine is for fresh wineskins."

*I*t is unsettling that John the Baptist's disciples are lumped together with the Pharisees in this account. Since John's arrest, are they gravitating toward a popular movement in order to regain security? Do they have something in common with the Pharisees? This is not the only time the two groups are spoken of together (see Lk 5:33). Perhaps, like the Pharisees, John's followers had begun to fast twice a week (Lk 18:12). The question comes to Jesus simply from the "people." Is Jesus' lack of orthodoxy beginning to disturb the community at large? Jesus responds with three brief parables.

First, he asks how the guests at the banquet can fast while the bridegroom is present. The unspoken answer: it would be inappropriate to refrain from the feast. But, says Jesus ominously, the time is coming when the bridegroom will be taken away. Then they will fast.

He abruptly shifts to the image of sewing a patch of new cloth on an old garment. The assumption again: such a thing would be inappropriate. New cloth will shrink and tear the old cloth. Just as abruptly, Jesus shifts the image again. Now he is asking them to picture an old, cracked wineskin and the absurd notion of pouring new wine into it. Again, the image is one of inappropriateness. New wine expands; old wineskins do not. You don't fast at a banquet, you don't sew new cloth on old, nor do you pour new wine into old wineskins.

The first image is the most clear and direct. Jesus is the bridegroom who will someday be taken away. His followers do not fast now because it would be inappropriate. The second and third images are less direct. The good news of Jesus cannot simply be stitched over the old tear in traditional orthodoxy. Neither can the old wineskins of ritual observance contain the new wine of the gospel. Old orthodoxy equals a worn-out garment and stiff old wineskins. The new reality equals fresh, clean cloth and new wine.

The purpose of fasting is to heighten awareness of God's presence so one can pray and be more sensitive to his voice. If this is its true purpose, then fasting in Jesus' presence has become irrelevant, even inappropriate. In time, when he is absent, it will become vital. Jesus is not anti-fasting. But he is in favor of a festive meal while he is present!

LORD OVER ORTHODOXY

²³On the Sabbath He was going through the grainfields, and His disciples began to make their way picking some heads of grain. ²⁴The Pharisees said to Him, "Look, why are they doing what is not lawful on the Sabbath?"

²⁵He said to them, "Have you never read what David and those who were with him did when he was in need and hungry—²⁶how he entered the house of God in the time of Abiathar the high priest and ate the sacred bread—which is not lawful for anyone to eat except the priests—and also gave some to his companions?" ²⁷Then He told them, "The Sabbath was made for man and not man for the Sabbath. ²⁸Therefore, the Son of Man is Lord even of the Sabbath."

*T*hroughout this series of stories of controversy, tension has risen. First, the scribes in Peter's house question Jesus, but only silently to themselves. Next, with Jesus' inappropriate choice of Levi, the Pharisees protest vocally. Regarding the issue of fasting, there is a brief lull as Jesus responds. Mark chooses not to tell us what the response of the people might have been. In the final two stories, Jesus violates the heart of orthodox observance: the Sabbath. By the end of this block, in Mark 3:6, the controversy will give birth to the plot to kill Jesus!

This is only the second time Mark has mentioned the Sabbath. In the first episode, in the synagogue in Capernaum (see Mk 1:21), there is no mention of any violation of the law. But now in the grainfields of Galilee, the first Sabbath infringement occurs.

Having left everything to follow Jesus, the disciples will naturally go hungry from time to time (see Mk 3:20; 8:1). Now, as they're traveling along, they help themselves to some heads of standing grain with the permission of Deuteronomy 23:25. The Pharisees' interpretation of Exodus 34:21 is scrupulous, and they see in the disciples' actions a glaring violation of the Sabbath. In their eyes, to pick grain is harvesting, an act of work. But Deuteronomy 23 clearly states that plucking grain is permitted; you are not allowed to use the sickle, which is clearly harvesting.

Jesus responds to the Pharisees by using the phrase "Have you never read . . ." (Mk 2:25), a technique common in rabbinic dialogue. He brings up a frequently debated passage, 1 Samuel 21, which contains a story from the life of David. When David and his companions were hungry, they ate consecrated bread in clear violation of the law. The bread was supposed to be eaten only by the priest. Jesus is drawing a line in the sand.

In Pharisaism, man was a slave to the Sabbath and observance became a burden instead of a joy. Jesus' statement (found only in Mark) that the "Sabbath was made for man and not man for the Sabbath" (Mk 2:27) is a scalpel he wields to cut out the tumor of heresy. Like David's companions, Jesus' friends are hungry and on a mission. Their need for life-sustaining food takes precedence over a questionable interpretation.

If Jesus had stopped there, the scene might have remained a stale-mate of one interpretation against another. But his conclusion in Mark 2:28 makes it crystal clear: this is not an issue of niggling interpreta-tion. It is a matter of divine authority and lordship. Jesus, the Son of Man, is master (*kurios*) of the Sabbath. He is Lord over orthodoxy—even the most sacred objects of orthodoxy, which the Sabbath was for the Pharisees. Lordship by definition knows no boundaries. There is no area of our lives where he is not master. Jesus' proclamation of lord-ship should cause us to stop and take account. We need to realize that whatever the facet of our orthodox observance, no matter how correct or biblical, he claims lordship even over that.

MARK 3

Discipling the Disciples

SABBATH OBSERVANCE

3:1-6 Jesus violates the oral law.

WHAT CAN'T BE KEPT SECRET

3:7-12 The crowd pursues Jesus.

THE CALL

3:13-19 The Twelve are appointed.

FUNDAMENTAL RECOGNITION

3:20-34 Jesus in conflict with scribes and family.

SABBATH OBSERVANCE

¹Now He entered the synagogue again, and a man was there who had a paralyzed hand. ²In order to accuse Him, they were watching Him closely to see whether He would heal him on the Sabbath. ³He told the man with the paralyzed hand, "Stand before us." ⁴Then He said to them, "Is it lawful on the Sabbath to do good or to do evil, to save life or to kill?" But they were silent. ⁵After looking around at them with anger and sorrow at the hardness of their hearts, He told the man, "Stretch out your hand." So he stretched it out, and his hand was restored. ⁶Immediately the Pharisees went out and started plotting with the Herodians against Him, how they might destroy Him.

cMark 3 opens with Jesus once more in the synagogue. The specific location is not given, but the detail that he was there "again" indicates that he has returned to Capernaum. Mark is not primarily concerned with location or chronology. In his grouping of stories of controversy, this is the final one in Galilee. This group will be balanced by five more controversy narratives once Jesus gets to Jerusalem.

The nameless, wordless man who appears in verse 1 is a silent cipher. As in almost every miracle account, the healing of the shriveled hand is not the point. There is a deeper miracle behind the visible miracle.

It is vital to understand the flow of Jesus' ministry at this moment. The conflict, which began in Mark 2:6 with a few scribes wondering to themselves if Jesus' words were appropriate, intensifies with the calling of Levi and Jesus' "unsatisfactory" answers to questions about fasting. At the end of chapter 2 we have Jesus' first verifiable Sabbath violation. Now, in Mark 3:2, the Pharisees are looking for a reason to accuse him, wondering if he will violate the Sabbath once more. The beginning of the plot to kill Jesus is only four verses away.

Jesus calls the man with the shriveled hand to stand up. As usual he begins the confrontation with a question rooted in rabbinic tradition. The rabbis used one test to determine if an exception might be made to the mandate for strenuous abstinence from work on the Sabbath. Simply put, it was, "Which way preserves life?" (the Mishnah,

Yoma 8:6; see also 1 Macc 2:41). This is what Jesus asks in Mark 3:4. True to form, the religious leaders have no answer. In verse 5 Mark's portrayal of the emotional life of Jesus comes into focus. He looks over the audience with a range of emotions. First he is angry (*orgēs*), then deeply sorrowful (*syllypeō*). The second term is found only here in the New Testament.

When Luke tells the same story, he is silent in regard to Jesus' state of mind. He does, however, inform us that the Pharisees were filled with rage (*anoia*; see Lk 6:11). Only Mark gives us the detail of Jesus' emotional reaction. At first the Pharisees' theological nitpicking angers him. They are setting another trap. The next instant he is grieved. They will be blind to a divine miracle, only seeing an infraction of one of their rules. A man is about to be made whole. Their stubborn hearts will remain shriveled. It is one of the unmiraculous miracles. There is no pronouncement, no waving of hands in the air, only three words in Greek, four in translation: "Stretch out your hand" (Mk 3:5).

Historians are not certain of the identity of the Herodians mentioned in Mark 3:6. Were they a political faction left over from the dynasty of Herod the Great? Were they in league with the current Herod Antipas? Or, as scholars have come to think more recently, was "Herodian" a local name applied to the Essenes, who received special favor from Herod the Great? We do not know for sure, but what is significant is that a coalition is forming against Jesus. A plot to take his life has begun, and it is only the third chapter of Mark.

WHAT CAN'T BE KEPT SECRET

⁷Jesus departed with His disciples to the sea, and a large crowd followed from Galilee, Judea, ⁸Jerusalem, Idumea, beyond the Jordan, and around Tyre and Sidon. The great multitude came to Him because they heard about everything He was doing. ⁹Then He told His disciples to have a small boat ready for Him, so the crowd would not crush Him. ¹⁰Since He had healed many, all who had diseases were pressing toward Him to touch Him. ¹¹Whenever the unclean spirits saw Him, those possessed fell down before Him and cried out, "You are the Son of God!" ¹²And He would strongly warn them not to make Him known.

*cA*fter verse 6 there is a break in the story from the synagogue community and organized Judaism in general. At the same point in the narrative, Matthew 12:15 tells us Jesus withdrew because he was aware of the plot to take his life. For Mark, it is simply a repetition of the pattern: confrontation and then retreat to the wilderness. The ever-present crowd is there, only it has grown significantly larger. Sidon is approximately sixty miles northwest of Galilee. Jerusalem is one hundred miles north. The people are coming from a much larger radius. In verse 9, Jesus must take the precaution of having a boat ready in case the crowd forces him into the lake. They push forward just to touch him. Those who are demon-possessed are shouting his true identity at the top of their lungs, and the emotional Jesus is "strongly warning" them to keep quiet.

The foundation of the ministry of Jesus has been laid. A fundamental break with organized religion has occurred; he will appear in the synagogue only once more (Mk 6:1-6). And no matter how much Jesus tries to avoid it, his popularity is getting out of control.

THE CALL

¹³Then He went up the mountain and summoned those He wanted, and they came to Him. ¹⁴He also appointed 12—He also named them apostles— to be with Him, to send them out to preach, ¹⁵and to have authority to drive out demons.

¹⁶He appointed the Twelve:
To Simon, He gave the name Peter;

¹⁷and to James the son of Zebedee,
and to his brother John,
He gave the name "Boanerges"
(that is, "Sons of Thunder");

¹⁸Andrew;
Philip and Bartholomew;
Matthew and Thomas;

James the son of Alphaeus,
and Thaddaeus;
Simon the Zealot,

¹⁹ and Judas Iscariot,
who also betrayed Him.

*J*esus moves to higher ground and calls a few of his followers to come with him. In isolation he sets twelve of them aside. It is a meaningful Old Testament number, connected to the covenant. From this moment in Mark's Gospel they are no longer simply "learners" or disciples. From now on they are the Twelve. Jesus appoints them as his "sent ones" (*apostoloi*). They will spend a period of concentrated time with him receiving special instruction. Then they will be sent out to preach his word and do his work.

The Synoptic Gospels, Matthew, Mark and Luke, all provide a list of the disciples. But Mark's is more personal. He provides more examples of what might be considered nicknames. This is certainly due to the fact that Peter is Mark's source. Simon's new name, "Peter," comes first, as it does in all lists of the Twelve. Then Jacob (James) and John. They receive a combined nickname: "Boanerges," or "Sons of Thunder," due to their hot-temperedness (see Lk 9:54). Next is Andrew, Peter's brother, an original follower of John the Baptist. Then Philip, who may have been a disciple of John's as well. Then Bartholomew, of whom we know absolutely nothing except that his father's name was Tolmai. Next, the "Gift of Yahweh," or Matthew.

Then comes Thomas, who has a nickname Mark apparently never heard about. In John's Gospel he is called "Didymus," or "the twin" (Jn 11:16; 20:24). Legend says he got this name because of his resemblance to Jesus. Next on the list is Matthew's brother Jacob (or James). Then two more possible nicknames: Thaddaeus, which means "bighearted" (Luke calls him "Judas"; Lk 6:16), and Simon, the "Zealot." This name is based on the Hebrew word *qana'*, "to be zealous." Traditionally Simon has been associated with the radical political movement of the same name.

The problem is that the Zealots did not come together until after the time of Jesus, during the revolt against Rome that ended in A.D. 70 with the destruction of the temple. If this is correct, then "the Zealot" may very well be another nickname.[5]

Finally we come to Judas, who is always last in the lists. The title "Iscariot" has been hotly debated. Is he Ishkerioth, the man (*ish*) from the village of Kerioth, some thirty miles from Jerusalem? Or is he Ish-sicarii, the "man of the sicar," a group of political assassins known for their use of a special dagger called a sicar? The Sicarii were founded in A.D. 6 in Galilee by another man named Judas. Or is there perhaps a third option? Might this be yet another nickname connected to some dark aspect of his character? Was he Judas, the "knife man"?

Whether any of these theories can be proved or not, do not overlook the last phrase of the list. Looking ahead two and a half to three years in time, Mark says Judas "also betrayed Him" (Mk 3:19). Conflict with religious leaders, a break from the religious norms of the day, a suffocating crowd that follows him everywhere with its bottomless need, and now, among his closest friends, a traitor.

FUNDAMENTAL RECOGNITION

[20]Then He went home, and the crowd gathered again so that they were not even able to eat. [21]When His family heard this, they set out to restrain Him, because they said, "He's out of His mind."

[22]The scribes who had come down from Jerusalem said, "He has Beelzebul in Him!" and, "He drives out demons by the ruler of the demons!"

[23]So He summoned them and spoke to them in parables: "How can Satan drive out Satan? [24]If a kingdom is divided against itself, that kingdom cannot stand. [25]If a house is divided against itself, that house cannot stand. [26]And if Satan rebels against himself and is divided, he cannot stand but is finished!

[27]"On the other hand, no one can enter a strong man's house and rob his possessions unless he first ties up the strong man. Then he will rob his house. [28]I assure you: People will be forgiven for all sins and whatever blasphemies they may blaspheme. [29]But whoever blasphemes against the Holy Spirit never has forgiveness, but is guilty of an eternal sin"—[30]because they were saying, "He has an unclean spirit."

³¹Then His mother and His brothers came, and standing outside, they sent word to Him and called Him. ³²A crowd was sitting around Him and told Him, "Look, Your mother, Your brothers, and Your sisters are outside asking for You."

³³He replied to them, "Who are My mother and My brothers?" ³⁴And looking about at those who were sitting in a circle around Him, He said, "Here are My mother and My brothers! ³⁵Whoever does the will of God is My brother and sister and mother."

*I*n this final section of chapter 3 Mark uses a bookend structure. He begins the story with Jesus' family's concern for his sanity in verses 20-21. Then in verses 22-30, he inserts Jesus' conflict with an investigative committee sent all the way from Jerusalem. Finally in verses 31-35, Mark provides the final bookend as Jesus' family arrives hoping to take him away from the crowd.

The first bookend (Mk 3:20-21) tells us that Jesus has returned to Capernaum, his new home. Again the crowd has inundated the ministry. So consuming are their demands that Jesus and his disciples do not even take the time to eat. Given the reports circulating about Jesus—his many conflicts, his break from the synagogue and now his refusal to take time to eat—his family is understandably concerned and decide that enough is enough. "He is out of his mind," or perhaps "He is beside himself," they conclude. After a family meeting, they are on their way, traveling approximately twenty-five miles from Nazareth to Capernaum to take Jesus away from the demanding crowd and back home where he will be safe.

In verse 22 we have a quick cut back to Capernaum. An investigative committee has traveled a hundred miles from Jerusalem. It seems they have already come to a conclusion; Jesus is in league with demonic powers. They believe he has aligned himself with the prince of demons, known as Beelzebul, originally "the exalted lord Baal." Later rabbinic texts refer to him as Baalzeboub, the Lord of the flies.[6]

Engage with your imagination. Grasp Jesus' bleak situation. The two groups from which he has a right to expect support, his family and the leaders of the religious community, have determined that he is insane and demon-possessed. Jesus goes on the defensive, using parables as his weapon of choice.

A kingdom or a house cannot stand if it is divided against itself, he says. Similarly, Satan is finished if he rebels against himself. It is an argument based on simple logic. If a strong man's house is going to be robbed the way Jesus is currently ripping off Satan's possessions, he would have to be tied up first. In this parable Jesus portrays himself as the robber. He has bound Satan in humiliating defeat.

Mark 3:28-29 contains the pronouncement that has regrettably been called the "unpardonable sin." Jesus begins the statement mysteriously; literally the Greek reads "amen." There is no precedent for it anywhere in the ancient writings. "Amen" is a traditional formula of response; an individual or congregation responds to a message by saying "amen" in agreement (see Rev 5:14). Paul uses it frequently to close his benedictions (see Rom 15:33; Gal 1:5; 6:18; 1 Tim 1:17) as does Peter (1 Pet 4:11; 5:11; 2 Pet 3:18). But the frequent double use of the word to initiate a pronouncement is unique to Jesus and has never been fully explained. This is the first time it occurs in the Gospel of Mark. It is meant to command our attention.

Jesus' pronouncement of the so-called unpardonable sin is based on the accusation from the Jerusalem contingent that he himself is possessed (Mk 3:30). Jesus is describing what they have just done to him. All sins will be forgiven, he says—even whatever they may blaspheme. But to blaspheme the Holy Spirit places a person beyond all forgiveness. If a person denies the vehicle of forgiveness (the Holy Spirit), he has cut himself off from the possibility of being forgiven. It is not the "unpardonable" sin. It is a sin whereby you place yourself beyond pardon.

In verses 31-35 Mark introduces the final bookend. As the color is draining from the faces of the Jerusalem scribes, Jesus' family arrives at the door. They send word inside, hoping Jesus will come out to them and lessen the embarrassment of having to take him into custody. But Jesus does not go out to them. He does not answer the call of his own mother! The crowd at his feet reiterates the urgency in Mark 3:32. Respect and care for one's parents (especially for a widowed mother) was enormously important in orthodox Judaism. Had there been tension in the family before? John's Gospel hints at conflict between Jesus and his unbelieving brothers (Jn 7:3-7). As the question hangs in the air, Jesus looks at the crowd packed around his feet. "Here is my family," he says with a sweep of his hand—"whoever does the will of God."

He has been cut off from his religious moorings, accused of being in league with demonic forces. At this moment he sits starving, not having taken the time to eat. He knows that his family has come, but now, Jesus says, he has a new family.

MARK 4

The Second Stage
of Galilean Ministry

THE PARADIGM PARABLE
(A SEED PARABLE)

4:1-20 Jesus teaches with parables.

THE NATURE OF LIGHT

4:21-25 A lamp is for light.

MORE SEED PARABLES

4:26-34 The mystery of the buried seed.

A GREAT WIND, A GREAT CALM
AND A GREAT FEAR

4:35-41 A demonic attack.

THE PARADIGM PARABLE (A SEED PARABLE)

[1] Again He began to teach by the sea, and a very large crowd gathered around Him. So He got into a boat on the sea and sat down, while the whole crowd was on the shore facing the sea. [2] He taught them many things in parables, and in His teaching He said to them: [3] "Listen! Consider the sower who went out to sow. [4] As he sowed, this occurred: Some seed fell along the path, and the birds came and ate it up. [5] Other seed fell on rocky ground where it didn't have much soil, and it sprang up right away, since it didn't have deep soil. [6] When the sun came up, it was scorched, and since it didn't have a root, it withered. [7] Other seed fell among thorns, and the thorns came up and choked it, and it didn't produce a crop. [8] Still others fell on good ground and produced a crop that increased 30, 60, and 100 times [what was sown]." [9] Then He said, "Anyone who has ears to hear should listen!"

[10] When He was alone with the Twelve, those who were around Him asked Him about the parables. [11] He answered them, "The secret of the kingdom of God has been given to you, but to those outside, everything comes in parables [12] so that

> *they may look and look,*
> *yet not perceive;*
> *they may listen and listen,*
> *yet not understand;*
> *otherwise, they might turn back—*
> *and be forgiven."*

[13] Then He said to them: "Don't you understand this parable? How then will you understand any of the parables? [14] The sower sows the word. [15] These are the ones along the path where the word is sown: when they hear, immediately Satan comes and takes away the word sown in them. [16] And these are the ones sown on rocky ground: when they hear the word, immediately they receive it with joy. [17] But they have no root in themselves; they are short-lived. When pressure or persecution comes because of the word, they immediately stumble. [18] Others are sown among thorns; these are the ones who hear the word, [19] but the worries of this age, the seduction of wealth, and the desires for other things enter in and choke the word, and it becomes unfruitful. [20] But the ones sown on good ground are those who

hear the word, welcome it, and produce a crop: 30, 60, and 100 times [what was sown]."

 *A*s the flow of the ministry proceeds into chapter 4, we find Jesus outdoors once more. Matthew 13:1 implies that he simply stepped outside the house and made his way to the shore. Earlier, he had asked that a boat be kept ready in case he needed it (Mk 3:9). Now he does! To maintain some degree of personal space, he sits in the boat and teaches the massive crowd on the shore.

To suggest Jesus did this to improve the acoustics is to miss the flow of the ministry. Yes, sound does carry better over water, but this is the eighth time the size of the crowd has been mentioned in Mark. From this point on, with few exceptions (e.g., Mk 6:2), he will be ministering outside. Along with the Olivet discourse of chapter 13, the seed parables represent the largest block of teaching in Mark's Gospel. It has been edited. Verse 2 says he taught "many things." We should understand that this session is representative of how Jesus taught.

He begins with a parable. Until now his parables have been primarily defensive, but the seed parables open new doors for us—if we will only listen. The first parable is unique in many ways. It is the only one that both opens and closes with the command to "listen!" It is crucial that the disciples understand this parable; if they don't, they won't understand any parable (Mk 3:13). It is a parable about how parables are understood. It is a parable about sowing seed, and as Jesus is speaking it, he is doing it.

He says nothing to prepare the audience apart from the command to listen. There are no opening jokes, no small talk, no hints to prepare them for what is to come. The crowd packed along the shoreline, filled with farmers from rural Galilee, would have immediately grasped the image. I imagine that on one of the nearby hillsides, a farmer is actually sowing seed. What happens to the seed in Jesus' story is what happens to seed in the real world:

- Some falls on the path and is eaten by birds. (It is crucial to understand that in the ancient world, the seed was sown first, then plowed into the soil.)

- Some falls on rocky soil and comes up quickly, but just as quickly it withers in the sun.
- Some falls among weeds and is choked out.
- Some falls on rich ground and thrives.

Then—and you and I should be shocked by this—it is all over. Jesus concludes with a command to hear: "Anyone who has ears to hear should listen!" (Mk 4:9). It is the first time that phrase is used in Mark. There is no public explanation. The crowd is left with the story. That is all. This is the greatest strength as well as the greatest weakness of Jesus' parables. If we do not engage, we will not "get it." The parables demand interaction. By their very nature they reveal the character of the person who listens (or doesn't listen) to them. Parables do what Jesus' story just said they do, and if this parable is accurate, it points to three times more failure than success.

In chapter 3 Jesus called and appointed the Twelve as the ones he would send. From this point until Mark 6:6 he will be preparing them. In a matter of days or weeks they too will go out and sow the seed of the word. It is crucial that they understand this foundational parable. In verse 10 of chapter 4 Mark cuts to a private moment. Jesus and the disciples are alone. Perhaps because Jesus was so adamant that the crowd hear and understand, the disciples are worried. They do not understand.

Jesus' tone shifts. Imagine him almost whispering. The secrets of the kingdom are going to be given to them; Jesus is about to explain the parable. He quotes a passage from Isaiah chapter 6. This is a rare example of a saying of Jesus that is quoted in all four Gospels (Mk 4:12; Mt 13:13; Lk 8:10; Jn 9:39).

Mark abbreviates the opening phrase, "so that." It implies the more complete statement "so that the prophecy will be fulfilled" (see Mt 13:14). When people listen (or not) to the parables of Jesus, at that moment, Isaiah's prophecy is being fulfilled. Here it's important to understand the context of Isaiah. His words were spoken in light of Israel's stubborn refusal to listen to God's Word. The ones who looked but didn't see and listened but didn't understand willfully chose to do so. Like those in Mark 3:29 who blaspheme the Holy Spirit, those who refuse to listen effectively place themselves beyond forgiveness. They deny the means; they refuse to cross the only bridge. Otherwise "they might turn back—and be forgiven."

Jesus does not tell demanding parables so that people will be cut off from forgiveness. If he is perfect, his words are perfect, the perfect means to communicate the truth of the Gospel. Jesus wants the ones he will send out to understand that as they speak the Word, like Isaiah they will encounter those who refuse to listen. It is an object of prophecy. And it fits perfectly into the flow of the ministry. In the remaining verses, Jesus does for the disciples what he will never do for the crowd—he unpacks the parable.

The seed is the Word; the people are the soil. The point of the parable is that there are different kinds of soil—perhaps it should be called the "parable of the soils." Some people are the soil along the path. The birds are Satan, who swoops in and, because of the listeners' stubborn refusal to hear, takes the seed away. Others are the poor, rocky soil. The seed sprouts but, because of the people's stubborn refusal to hear, they fall away. Mark 4:17 provides a window into Mark's listening audience in Rome, believers who were facing persecution under the emperor Nero. Only Mark speaks of persecution that "comes because of the word." His first readers would have paid attention. Persecution should not cause them to stop listening and nurturing the seed planted in their hearts.

Next, those represented by the soil that grows thorns are warned not to let the worries of the world choke out the word planted in their lives. Greed is a seed in and of itself. It produces weeds and thorns of disbelief. Finally comes the good soil that represents those who are willing to listen. They look and perceive, they listen and understand, and so cross over and find forgiveness. The crop they yield is extraordinarily fruitful.

THE NATURE OF LIGHT

[21] He also said to them, "Is a lamp brought in to be put under a basket or

under a bed? Isn't it to be put on a lampstand? ²²For nothing is concealed except to be revealed, and nothing hidden except to come to light. ²³If anyone has ears to hear, he should listen!" ²⁴Then He said to them, "Pay attention to what you hear. By the measure you use, it will be measured and added to you. ²⁵For to the one who has, it will be given, and from the one who does not have, even what he has will be taken away."

*A*s the private discussion with the disciples continues, Jesus shifts the lesson. He talks about light. In case some of them have not understood the parable of the seed (and it is always safe to assume some haven't), Jesus talks about the nature of truth and its inherent ability to shine.

Lights are meant to illuminate, to be set up on stands. Then they reveal what is otherwise hidden in the darkness. The purpose of the parables is the same. They are perfect vehicles for illumination. By their very nature, they shine. But there will always be those who shove them under beds or cover them up with bowls.

"Pay attention to what you hear," Jesus says in Mark 4:24, repeating his theme. It is all about listening and seeing, understanding and perceiving. The parables speak, they shine; the Word has power of its own and grows. Our response, the measure of attention we use, means everything. If we genuinely give ear, more will be measured out to us. If we stubbornly refuse to engage, even what we have will be taken away. This is not a statement on the character of Jesus, who longs for everyone to come to salvation. It is a statement about the nature of truth and the consequences of refusing to listen.

MORE SEED PARABLES

²⁶*"The kingdom of God is like this," He said. "A man scatters seed on the ground; ²⁷he sleeps and rises—night and day, and the seed sprouts and grows—he doesn't know how. ²⁸The soil produces a crop by itself—first the blade, then the head, and then the ripe grain on the head. ²⁹But as soon as the crop is ready, he sends for the sickle, because the harvest has come."*

³⁰*And He said: "How can we illustrate the kingdom of God, or what par-*

able can we use to describe it? ³¹It's like a mustard seed that, when sown in the soil, is smaller than all the seeds on the ground. ³²And when sown, it comes up and grows taller than all the vegetables, and produces large branches, so that the birds of the sky can nest in its shade."

³³He would speak the word to them with many parables like these, as they were able to understand. ³⁴And He did not speak to them without a parable. Privately, however, He would explain everything to His own disciples.

*H*aving outlined the nature of understanding and the demand to engage, Jesus tells two more parables about seed. He is like a musician improvising, expanding on his original theme. In verse 26 he begins a parable about the mysterious nature of a seed's power. Once again a man is scattering seed, just as the disciples will soon go out to spread the word. After he is done sowing, the seed takes over. As children we may have planted small seeds in milk cartons and watched as they mysteriously grew on their own. We would come to class and discover first a shoot, then a few days later a full-grown plant.

Jesus speaks of the seed having power of its own. After it has been sown in the ground, it will grow no matter what you do. He wants his disciples to have confidence in the self-contained power of the seed. As it is the nature of light to shine, even so it is the nature of the seed to grow and produce a crop. The disciples must learn to trust the power of the message they are spreading. Otherwise they might be tempted to explain away the parable and rob it of its power. Though they will meet with difficulties on the road, stubborn disbelief and refusal to listen, they should have faith that some of the seed is falling on fertile ground. The Word has power all its own and will yield results in time.

As their private time of instruction comes to a close, Jesus tells one more seed parable. If he were trying to be obscure, as he is sometimes said to be in this passage, he would not tell the same truth from three different perspectives. The final parable of the tiny mustard seed is an extension of the previous parable; it is another improvisation on the earlier theme. In this parable Jesus accentuates the truth that the size of the seed has nothing to do with its power.

The mustard seed and its tiny size is one of Jesus' favorite images (see Mt 17:20). It is clear that as he engaged with the natural world, Jesus learned its lessons and wove them into his teaching. If you have ever held a single mustard seed, as small as a grain of sand, you have most likely been amazed that an enormous shrub could grow from it. The kingdom is like that, Jesus says. It is another reason to have confidence in the seed. Even though the disciples on mission will constantly face obstacles of every kind, they must trust the nature of the gospel. It has its own power. Like the minute mustard seed, it may seem pitifully small in the beginning, but history shows that the Word multiplies and spreads and grows to unimaginable proportions.

It is a profound word of encouragement to those who go out to sow. If we engage with our imaginations as we listen, we will hear the tone of encouragement in Jesus' voice. If you are a parent with a wayward child in whom you planted the gospel, then trust the seed. It has power of its own. Are you a pastor, youth worker or missionary struggling in the face of what seems an unfruitful ministry? Trust the seed, the self-contained power of the Word, which will not return empty.

As the teaching time comes to a close, Mark tells us this has been just a small taste. Jesus told many other parables like these. He was careful to only tell as much as they could understand. His parables were told in order to be understood by those who would engage with their imaginations. Only Mark tells us all of the seed parables. With Peter as his source, he was especially sensitive to the fact that Jesus was discipling his own disciples, preparing them for their upcoming mission of sowing the good news of the gospel.

A GREAT WIND, A GREAT CALM
AND A GREAT FEAR

35 On that day, when evening had come, He told them, "Let's cross over to the other side [of the lake]." 36 So they left the crowd and took Him along since He was [already] in the boat. And other boats were with Him. 37 A fierce windstorm arose, and the waves were breaking over the boat, so that the boat was already being swamped. 38 But He was in the stern, sleeping on the cush-

ion. So they woke Him up and said to Him, "Teacher! Don't you care that we're going to die?"

³⁹He got up, rebuked the wind, and said to the sea, "Silence! Be still!" The wind ceased, and there was a great calm. ⁴⁰Then He said to them, "Why are you fearful? Do you still have no faith?"

⁴¹And they were terrified and asked one another, "Who then is this? Even the wind and the sea obey Him!"

*M*ark has made it clear at the outset that Jesus' presence causes an outpouring of demonic activity around him. Everywhere he goes he is confronted by demonized people who disrupt his ministry by crying out who he is. Jesus continually tells them to "be muzzled." As the intense time of the disciples' preparation comes to a close, Jesus informs them that they will now proceed to the other side of the lake. Once they've crossed over, another demoniac will challenge them. But in crossing the lake they encounter an even more serious attack.

First, let's make this clear: the Gospels tell of two storms on the Sea of Galilee. The second (Mk 6:45) is merely a contrary wind. Jesus will walk on the waves to reach his exhausted disciples. This first storm is a completely different matter. The disciples, many of whom are seasoned fisherman who grew up on the lake, have seen all sorts of storms. But they have never seen anything like this.

Matthew refers to the storm as a "shaking" (*seismos*). Mark calls it a "great wind" (*megale anaemu*). It is a demonic attempt on their lives. Satan has Jesus and the disciples together in a single boat on the lake. It is his opportunity to wipe out the ministry in a single stroke. It has all the hallmarks of a demonic attack.

The Sea of Galilee is a freshwater lake. Though it is enormous (thirteen miles long and eight miles wide), you can always see the other side. It is one of the lowest points on earth, seven hundred feet below sea level. Many commentaries refer to weather patterns in and around the lake. They observe that frequent and sudden storms happen all the time. But the violence of this storm has nothing to do with meteorology.

A "fierce windstorm" attacks the small group of boats. Mark says that the one carrying Jesus and his disciples is "swamped." So exhausted is Jesus from the difficult days leading up to this moment that he has collapsed, sound asleep in the stern on a cushion. (Note that Jonah, another prophet from Galilee, also slept in the midst of a demonic storm; see Jonah 1:5-6.) The person in the position of steering the ship is asleep! The disciples become unhinged.

So Jesus speaks to the storm the same words he speaks to silence demons: "Be muzzled!" (see Mk 1:25). In an instant Mark's great wind becomes a "great calm." We might expect from Mark a few words on Jesus' emotions. But people who are roused from a deep sleep are rarely emotional. The question does hint that Jesus is puzzled. Why should they have been afraid? Have they not seen enough proof that Jesus has total command over the forces of darkness? Can they not trust him yet?

Mark is not silent about the disciples' emotions: "They were terrified" (Mk 4:41). The severe test of the storm has revealed that they still have no idea who Jesus really is. The great wind that attempted to claim all their lives has become a great calm. In the midst of the great calm, the Twelve experience a great fear. Whenever Jesus reveals himself in new ways, the result in the disciples is fear.

MARK 5

People at Jesus' Feet

AN UNQUALIFIED APOSTLE

5:1–20 The healing of the man from the tombs.

A DYING WOMAN

5:21–35 The touching of Jesus' shawl.

A DEAD DAUGHTER

5:36–43 The raising of Jarius's daughter.

AN UNQUALIFIED APOSTLE

¹Then they came to the other side of the sea, to the region of the Gerasenes. ²As soon as He got out of the boat, a man with an unclean spirit came out of the tombs and met Him. ³He lived in the tombs. No one was able to restrain him anymore—even with chains—⁴because he often had been bound with shackles and chains, but had snapped off the chains and smashed the shackles. No one was strong enough to subdue him. ⁵And always, night and day, he was crying out among the tombs and in the mountains and cutting himself with stones.

⁶When he saw Jesus from a distance, he ran and knelt down before Him. ⁷And he cried out with a loud voice, "What do You have to do with me, Jesus, Son of the Most High God? I beg You before God, don't torment me!" ⁸For He had told him, "Come out of the man, you unclean spirit!"

⁹"What is your name?" He asked him.

"My name is Legion," he answered Him, "because we are many." ¹⁰And he kept begging Him not to send them out of the region.

¹¹Now a large herd of pigs was there, feeding on the hillside. ¹²The demons begged Him, "Send us to the pigs, so we may enter them." ¹³And He gave them permission. Then the unclean spirits came out and entered the pigs, and the herd of about 2,000 rushed down the steep bank into the sea and drowned there. ¹⁴The men who tended them ran off and reported it in the town and the countryside, and people went to see what had happened. ¹⁵They came to Jesus and saw the man who had been demon-possessed by the legion, sitting there, dressed and in his right mind; and they were afraid. ¹⁶The eyewitnesses described to them what had happened to the demon-possessed man and [told] about the pigs. ¹⁷Then they began to beg Him to leave their region.

¹⁸As He was getting into the boat, the man who had been demon-possessed kept begging Him to be with Him. ¹⁹But He would not let him; instead, He told him, "Go back home to your own people, and report to them how much the Lord has done for you and how He has had mercy on you." ²⁰So he went out and began to proclaim in the Decapolis how much Jesus had done for him, and they were all amazed.

*E*ach individual described in Mark 5 is being held captive: one by demons, one by disease and one by death. In each situation Jesus will exercise the absolute authority we've seen throughout Mark's Gospel. It is important that we maintain an awareness of the flow of the ministry. Keep in mind that as Jesus and his disciples come ashore on the other side of the lake, they've just been through a demonic storm. I imagine the boat riding low in the water as waves splashed over the gunwales. The disciples have been terrified, first by the storm, then by Jesus' power.

The region of the Gerasenes lies on the eastern shore of the Sea of Galilee. It is in the area of the Decapolis, or the "ten cities." A nearby village is called Gadara, hence the "Gadarenes" in Matthew 8:28. This is a predominantly Gentile region, regarded by the Jews as a thorn in their side.

As Jesus gets out of the boat he is confronted by a man who is a poster child for demonic possession. He lives among the unclean tombs. He displays otherworldly strength. He wanders among the graves at night, howling. He cuts himself with stones (see 1 Kings 18:28). Once again, the presence of Jesus causes demonic forces to attack. This story is simply part two of the storm on the lake.

The man screams, first asking Jesus what he wants. Even the demons possessing the man must acknowledge that he is "Son of the Most High" (Mk 5:7; see also Jas 2:19). The next howling utterance is puzzling: they ask Jesus not to torture them. The demons may be afraid that Jesus will punish them for the earlier attack on the lake. When Matthew tells the story he gives a fuller quote: "Have You come here to torment us before the time?" (Mt 8:29). Demons must spend their days on earth knowing that a time has been appointed for their destruction (Rom 16:20; 2 Pet 2:4; Rev 19:20-21). Though their punishment awaits them, demons live a tortured existence in the present.

Jesus engages them by asking their name. In the context of spiritual warfare, knowing someone's name is supposed to give you power. In the very first confrontation in Mark's Gospel, the demon cries out to Jesus, "I know who You are!" (Mk 1:24). But Jesus' power is absolute. The fact that a demon knows his name does not give the demon any power. Similarly, in Mark 5:9, Jesus does not ask for the demon's name in order to gain power over it. He already has that power. Notice the confusion of the pronouns in the verse when the demon speaks: "*My* name is . . . for *we* are . . ." Is the wretched voice the man's or the demon's—or perhaps some of both?

"Legion" is a Roman military term describing a fighting force of two thousand to six thousand men. Beneath this name lies a threat. The demon is trying to imply that if a battle occurs, he has superior numbers. Other passages in the Gospels also speak of possession by multiple demons (Mt 12:45; Lk 8:2, 11:26). The threat soon dissolves, however, and the demons, sensing that their cause is helpless, beg to stay in the area. (One of the cities of the Decapolis, Hippos, was a city dedicated to demons.) Note that they must fully submit to Jesus' authority. They beg for permission to go, knowing that if it is Jesus' will, they must leave the man.

One clear indication that we are no longer in Jewish territory is the presence of the massive herd of unclean pigs on the nearby hillside. When the demons enter the pigs, the entire herd plunges headlong into the lake and drowns. I wonder if even in the drowning of the pigs Satan was trying to intimidate Jesus. What happened to the pigs was what he had intended for Jesus and the Twelve in the earlier attack in the storm.

The death of the pigs demonstrates the ultimate aim of demonic possession. The first purpose is to mar the image of God in the person possessed. This was pitifully evident in the man from the tombs. The second goal is death. What happened to the pigs was what would have eventually happened to the man.

But now the person who was howling, naked and bleeding only moments earlier is dressed and in his right mind. The local people have run to see for themselves and, like the disciples in the storm, they are afraid of what they find. The revelation of Jesus' absolute authority elicits fear. As a result they beg Jesus to leave. In Mark 5:18 he responds by getting back into his boat.

The man who had been possessed begs to go with Jesus. If Jesus' purpose were to attract a crowd, this man would certainly be a marvelous draw. But Jesus is not interested in drawing throngs of people and is not accepting volunteers (see Lk 9:57-58, 61-62). We must first be called by Jesus and respond to his call—the call that makes everything possible.

In Mark 5:19 Jesus does something he has not done before. He tells the man to go home and tell his family what happened. The fact that this is a Gentile area accounts for this departure from the norm. Few people in the Decapolis would have nurtured false ideas about the Messiah. When Jesus returns to this area in Mark 7:31-37, he will encounter people who have heard about his power. Though the man was not permitted to be one of the disciples, he was still allowed to serve as the first missionary to the Gentiles.

A DYING WOMAN

[21] When Jesus had crossed over again by boat to the other side, a large crowd gathered around Him while He was by the sea. [22] One of the synagogue leaders, named Jairus, came, and when he saw Jesus, he fell at His feet [23] and kept begging Him, "My little daughter is at death's door. Come and lay Your hands on her so she can get well and live."

[24] So Jesus went with him, and a large crowd was following and pressing against Him.

[25] A woman suffering from bleeding for 12 years [26] had endured much under many doctors. She had spent everything she had and was not helped at all. On the contrary, she became worse. [27] Having heard about Jesus, she came behind Him in the crowd and touched His robe. [28] For she said, "If I can just touch His robes, I'll be made well!" [29] Instantly her flow of blood ceased, and she sensed in her body that she was cured of her affliction.

[30] At once Jesus realized in Himself that power had gone out from Him. He turned around in the crowd and said, "Who touched My robes?"

[31] His disciples said to Him, "You see the crowd pressing against You, and You say, 'Who touched Me?'"

[32] So He was looking around to see who had done this. [33] Then the woman, knowing what had happened to her, came with fear and trembling, fell down before Him, and told Him the whole truth. [34] "Daughter," He said to her, "your faith has made you well. Go in peace and be free from your affliction."

*J*esus crisscrosses to the other side of the lake. He finds waiting for him the ever-present crowd. There he encounters the second person who will fall at his feet in this chapter. Mark tells us his name is Jairus, the chief official of the synagogue. He is responsible for overseeing the building and details of the services. None of the Gospels identify the exact location of the story. Perhaps Jesus has come back to Capernaum. This would be a meaningful detail, for the last time Jesus was in the Capernaum synagogue he met stiff opposition. But none of that means anything to Jairus. All he knows is that his daughter is dying and Jesus has the power to heal her.

As the mob following Jesus and Jairus makes its way into town, we encounter the third character of chapter 5. She is a woman who has experienced vaginal bleeding for twelve years. Mark tells us she has suffered a great deal as a result of the medical care she has received. When we read about what passed for medical care in Jesus' day, this woman's ordeal becomes clearer. One cure for bleeding was to fish an oak grain out of cattle dung and force the patient to swallow it. Not only did her condition worsen as a result of these "therapies," she was now broke, having spent all her money on doctors. Imagine a severely anemic woman, exhausted, desperate and at this moment afraid.

Why afraid? Because she has heard the rumor that if she can touch the fringe of Jesus' prayer shawl, she will be healed. But she knows that if she touches him and is discovered, she will be accused of rendering him unclean. Her bleeding has not simply made her weak and poor. In the context of first-century Judaism, she has been cut off from her community by ritual uncleanness that has lasted twelve years!

Under cover of the crowd's confusion, she makes her way to Jesus and touches his cloak. She immediately senses in her body that she is healed. Also "at once" Jesus senses the drain of his power (Mk 5:30). He doggedly sets out to find her, not satisfied that she has simply received his healing. Once again Mark is making it clear that Jesus did not come just to give his gifts. He came to give himself. At this moment, in all the confusion, the disciples speak disrespectfully to Jesus for the third time (Mk 5:31; see also Mk 1:37; 4:38).

Knowing she cannot get away, the woman comes to Jesus and falls at his feet. She is pale, trembling and afraid she will receive punishment for rendering him unclean. She begins to blurt out the sad details of her story only to hear Jesus' gentle response: "Daughter" (Mk 5:34). It is an affectionate family term, and this is the only time we hear Jesus use it. He deflects attention away from himself, saying that is it is her own faith that has healed her. But of course we know it was her faith in him.

A DEAD DAUGHTER

35While He was still speaking, people came from the synagogue leader's house and said, "Your daughter is dead. Why bother the Teacher anymore?"

36But when Jesus overheard what was said, He told the synagogue leader, "Don't be afraid. Only believe." 37He did not let anyone accompany Him except Peter, James, and John, James' brother. 38They came to the leader's house, and He saw a commotion—people weeping and wailing loudly. 39He went in and said to them, "Why are you making a commotion and weeping? The child is not dead but asleep."

40They started laughing at Him, but He put them all outside. He took the child's father, mother, and those who were with Him, and entered the place where the child was. 41Then He took the child by the hand and said to her, "Talitha koum!" (which is translated, "Little girl, I say to you, get up!"). 42Immediately the girl got up and began to walk. (She was 12 years old.) At this they were utterly astounded. 43Then He gave them strict orders that no one should know about this and said that she should be given something to eat.

*T*he delay must have seemed catastrophic for Jairus—especially when the men came to inform him that his daughter had died. Their statement, "Why bother the teacher anymore?" speaks volumes. Listen closely to the text. Behind their words lies a presupposition. When the child was sick, Jesus could heal her. They all believed that. Now she is dead and there is no need to bother Jesus any longer. They presume Jesus' power does not extend to raising the dead.

I have my own literal translation for Jesus' whispered response to

Jairus. I whisper it to myself whenever I'm afraid, whenever I am suffering my own false presuppositions about Jesus: "No fear, only faith."

As they make their way to Jairus's house, Jesus allows only Peter, James and John to follow him. This will not be a public display of his power. Very much in keeping with Mark's emphasis, Jesus will perform the healing in private. In Mark 5:43 he will again order that they keep the miracle a secret.

As the small group approaches the house they hear the wailing. Jesus asks why are they mourning for someone who is only asleep. In response, they laugh at him. The traditional explanation for this abrupt shift from wailing to laughter has been that the crowd was composed of professional mourners, a custom in the culture of Jesus' time. Since they were only under hire to wail and mourn, they could quickly transition to laughter. (I am increasingly dissatisfied with that explanation, but I have yet to find a better one.)

By my count, there are seven people in the room; the three disciples, the two parents, Jesus and the dead girl. This is a dramatic moment in the Gospel of Mark. It is the first time we hear Jesus speaking in his native tongue of Aramaic: "Talitha koum." It is tender, as his words to the bleeding woman were tender. "Little girl, I say to you get up!"

When Jesus refers to death as sleep, no one ever understands (see Jn 11:11). It is not a euphemism, it is a redefinition. In him death has become merely a sleep from which we will someday be awakened by the sound of his voice.

Three people fall at his feet. A frantic, demon-possessed man, a dying woman and a fearful father. All find exactly what they need at Jesus' feet.

MARK 6

Two Banquets

THE AMAZED JESUS

6:1–5 Jesus driven from Nazareth.

THE COMMISSION

6:6–13 The Twelve sent on a mission.

A PUZZLING WEALTH OF DETAIL

6:14–29 The murder of John the Baptist.

PERFECT PROVISION

6:30–44 The feeding of the five thousand.

THE INCOMPLETE STORY OF
THE WATER WALKER

6:45–56 The second storm on the lake.

THE AMAZED JESUS

¹He went away from there and came to His hometown, and His disciples followed Him. ²When the Sabbath came, He began to teach in the synagogue, and many who heard Him were astonished. "Where did this man get these things?" they said. "What is this wisdom given to Him, and how are these miracles performed by His hands? ³Isn't this the carpenter, the son of Mary, and the brother of James, Joses, Judas, and Simon? And aren't His sisters here with us?" So they were offended by Him.

⁴Then Jesus said to them, "A prophet is not without honor except in his hometown, among his relatives, and in his household." ⁵So He was not able to do any miracles there, except that He laid His hands on a few sick people and healed them. ⁶And He was amazed at their unbelief.

*T*his is the last time we will see Jesus in Nazareth. His home village, being only about ten acres in size with a population of around two hundred, is considerably smaller than his adopted home of Capernaum. This is also the last time we will see him in this or any synagogue. In verse 2, Mark tells us Jesus is teaching. But as we have come to expect by now, he neglects to give us the content of the lesson.

As the passage progresses it takes an abrupt, unexpected turn. At one moment the townspeople marvel at Jesus' wisdom, clearly a reference to his remarkable teaching and the fact that, unlike other rabbis, he never quoted another source. Then someone remembers that Jesus is a carpenter. The Greek word used, *tektōn*, indicates anyone with technical skill who works with wood or stone. Yet Jesus uses carpentry metaphors only rarely (see Mt 7:4). More frequently he employs building images (see Mt 7:24; 16:18; Mk 14:58; Lk 12:18, 14:29). Perhaps he was more involved in building houses and stone walls than small wooden objects.

Next the synagogue crowd makes the connection to Jesus' family. They recognize him as "the son of Mary" (Mk 6:3). The fact that Joseph is not mentioned is an indication that he has already died. His four brothers are named, and there is a reference to an unnumbered group of sisters. Jesus' brothers are occasionally mentioned in the New Testament, though it seems they were slow in coming to faith in him (see Jn 7:5). Later at least two of them, James and Jude, become active in the early church.

At once the townspeople are "offended" (Mk 6:3). That is, they stumble because Jesus has failed to meet their expectations (see Is 8:14; Rom 9:33; 1 Pet 2:8). The missing piece of the puzzle for this story might be found in Luke 4:16-30. Jesus is in the same Nazareth synagogue. He is asked to read a passage from the prophets at the close of the service, known as the *haphtarah*. He concludes by telling the crowd that that Scripture has been fulfilled this very day. As in Mark's account, initially the crowd is "amazed." At this point in Luke, someone recognizes that Jesus is "Joseph's son" (Lk 4:22).

Jesus responds with a brief sermon. He focuses on two instances from the Old Testament when God chose to bless Gentiles over Jews. By Luke's account, it is the sermon that has the people of Nazareth "enraged" (Lk 4:28). Though they intend to throw Jesus down a steep hill, he walks through the crowd and goes on his way.

I like to think these separate accounts from Mark and Luke, though appearing in different places on the timeline of Jesus' ministry, reflect the same occasion. Perhaps Luke has positioned the story closer to the beginning of Jesus' ministry in order to establish one of his major themes: the universality of the gospel. Even if they do recount separate incidents, one is relevant to understanding the other.

Mark brings the scene to a close with Jesus' observation that no prophet receives the honor due him in the midst of his relatives or in his own house. Jesus cannot bring himself to do any miracles there except lay hands on a few people and heal them. Now it is Jesus' turn to be "amazed." Of all that he understands, of all that he knows, Jesus is still astounded that the people he has known all his life refuse to believe. Indeed, only two things ever amaze Jesus: faith (Lk 7:9) or the lack thereof.

THE COMMISSION

⁶Now He was going around the villages in a circuit, teaching. ⁷He summoned the Twelve and began to send them out in pairs and gave them authority over unclean spirits. ⁸He instructed them to take nothing for the road

except a walking stick: no bread, no traveling bag, no money in their belts.
⁹They were to wear sandals, but not put on an extra shirt. ¹⁰Then He said to
them, "Whenever you enter a house, stay there until you leave that place. ¹¹If
any place does not welcome you and people refuse to listen to you, when you
leave there, shake the dust off your feet as a testimony against them."

¹²So they went out and preached that people should repent. ¹³And they
were driving out many demons, anointing many sick people with oil, and
healing.

*T*his story of the commissioning and sending of the Twelve is the
first of another of Mark's literary bookends. After this passage comes a
mysteriously lengthy account of the death of John the Baptist. Then
Mark gives us the second bookend, an account of the disciples' return
from their first mission.

Beginning with Mark 3:13-15, Jesus has been actively, even aggres-
sively, discipling his disciples. He has taken them on a series of hands-
on ministry experiences. They have seen Jesus in conflict with his own
family and with religious leaders. They have seen Jesus heal. They have
heard Jesus preach the Word. They have witnessed his power over demons. Now the time has come for the Twelve to be sent out on their
own mission.

As they gather around Jesus, he pairs them up so that their testimony will be established by the mouths of two witnesses (see Deut
17:6). Also, teams of two can better withstand the stresses and strains
of the road, and a team of two can encourage one another. To his "sent
ones," his apostles, his authoritative representatives, Jesus gives his authority over evil spirits. They are allowed only a staff, the clothes on
their backs (but no extra tunic) and a pair of shoes. They are to take no
money to provide them with food or shelter. They will completely depend on Jewish hospitality.

This has been Jesus' mode in ministry from the beginning. He
does not seem to have kept any money on his person (see Mk 12:15)
and he stays in private homes when he is on the road (see Mt 25:35;
Lk 10:38-42). This first mission extends exclusively to the Jewish

community, to the "lost sheep of the house of Israel" (Mt 10:6). When Jesus sends the disciples out for the final time, he will tell them to load up on provisions, even to purchase a sword if need be, for they will be going out into the world at large, staying in dangerous Gentile inns (Lk 22:35-37).

In Mark 6:10, Jesus instructs the Twelve to stay put in a single house when they're ministering to a certain community. They are not to be like beggars, going from door to door seeking food. They must realize that as his "sent ones" they bear a concealed dignity. They are going out in Jesus' name, speaking his Word and doing his work. Many towns will turn them away, the same way he has just been thrown out of his own hometown. They are not to respond in anger, only to shake the dust of that town off their feet (see Acts 13:51; 18:6). Jesus' commission to his disciples does not include the authority to pass judgment on the cities that turn them away. They are to leave that to God.

A PUZZLING WEALTH OF DETAIL

[14]King Herod heard of this, because Jesus' name had become well known. Some said, "John the Baptist has been raised from the dead, and that's why supernatural powers are at work in him." [15]But others said, "He's Elijah." Still others said, "He's a prophet—like one of the prophets."

[16]When Herod heard of it, he said, "John, the one I beheaded, has been raised! [17]For Herod himself had given orders to arrest John and to chain him in prison on account of Herodias, his brother Philip's wife, whom he had married. [18]John had been telling Herod, "It is not lawful for you to have your brother's wife!" [19]So Herodias held a grudge against him and wanted to kill him. But she could not, [20]because Herod was in awe of John and was protecting him, knowing he was a righteous and holy man. When Herod heard him he would be very disturbed, yet would hear him gladly.

[21]Now an opportune time came on his birthday, when Herod gave a banquet for his nobles, military commanders, and the leading men of Galilee. [22]When Herodias's own daughter came in and danced, she pleased Herod and his guests. The king said to the girl, "Ask me whatever you want, and I'll give it to you." [23]So he swore oaths to her: "Whatever you ask me I will give you, up to half my kingdom."

²⁴Then she went out and said to her mother, "What should I ask for?"
"John the Baptist's head!" she said.
²⁵Immediately she hurried to the king and said, "I want you to give me John the Baptist's head on a platter—right now!"
²⁶Though the king was deeply distressed, because of his oaths and the guests he did not want to refuse her. ²⁷The king immediately sent for an executioner and commanded him to bring John's head. So he went and beheaded him in prison, ²⁸brought his head on a platter, and gave it to the girl. Then the girl gave it to her mother. ²⁹When his disciples heard about it, they came and removed his corpse and placed it in a tomb.

*T*he story that Mark places between his two bookends comprises two scenes. The first, in Mark 6:14-16, explains that Jesus' third Galilean ministry tour has caused him to come onto Herod Antipas's radar screen. There have been confused rumors that Jesus might be John the Baptist raised from the dead. It is not hard to imagine how such confusion came about with Jesus actually raising Jarius's daughter from the dead. Most rumors contain a kernel of truth.

The second, far longer scene in Mark 6:17-29 portrays the cruel and meaningless death of Jesus' cousin John the Baptist. When we last heard about John, he had been arrested by Herod (Mk 1:14). And by this point it has been some time since Herod ordered John's execution. Now he concludes, in a moment of guilt and horror, that the man he murdered is alive and preaching once more in Galilee.

This story necessitates a bit of untangling. It requires that we take a closer look at the family of Herod, and that family tree is twisted, convoluted and confusing.

The Herod in this account, known as Herod Antipas, or simply Antipas, is the second son of Herod the Great, the tyrant who tried in vain to murder the infant Jesus (Mt 2:7-16). His mother, one of Herod the Great's multiple wives, was a Samaritan named Malthace. Antipas ruled the province of Galilee from 4 B.C. to A.D. 39. While visiting his half-brother Philip in Rome, he fell in love with his brother's wife, Herodias. Antipas divorced his first wife, the daughter of King Aretas

IV, setting off a border war between their two countries.

In addition to being the wife of Antipas's half-brother Philip, Herodias was the daughter of another half-brother, making her both Antipas's sister-in-law and niece. She eventually led to Antipas's downfall by coercing him to pressure the emperor Caligula to grant him the title of king. Caligula, himself a member of a twisted and convoluted family, was offended by the request and banished Antipas to Gaul in A.D. 39. Herodias, in the only act of loyalty we know about her, voluntarily accompanied her husband into exile.

Finally we come to Salome, who is not necessarily the young nubile pictured in the popular movie versions of the story. She is already a married woman. She is Herodias's daughter by her first marriage, which means she is Antipas's stepdaughter.[7]

As we already know from Mark 1:14, John is in prison. Josephus tells us he is in the Machaerus ("the black fortress") built by Alexander Jannaeus during the Maccabean revolt and later rebuilt by Herod the Great. It is located on the eastern shore of the Sea of Galilee. Its ruins contain two *triclinia*, or banqueting rooms. John is in prison for publicly speaking against Anitpas's adulterous marriage to his brother's wife. She must have been behind the arrest. Once John is in prison, Antipas is inclined to protect him. He must have liked to listen to John but was undoubtedly troubled by what he heard.

Herodias sees her chance during Antipas's birthday feast. A large group of important men have come together, perhaps including some of the Herodians who were plotting to kill Jesus in Mark 3:6. As part of the festivities, Antipas's stepdaughter Salome performs a dance. We are left to imagine what "she pleased his guests" might mean. If we consider the lifestyle of the family as a whole, their rejection of the value system of Judaism and the outcome of this particular incident, a strong case can be made that her performance was at least improper and most probably lewd in nature.

We can detect his inappropriate passion as Antipas promises to give Salome anything she wants. He is carried away by the dance. Salome understands that this is an opportunity her mother will want to seize. "What should I ask for?" she whispers, out of breath (Mk

6:24). Antipas does not see it coming. Salome, as a sick joke, not only acquiesces to her mother's demand for John's head but asks that it be served up on a platter, like another course at the banquet. Herod reluctantly complies. John's disciples come and bury the decapitated body. (If you're wondering how Mark came to know eyewitness details of the scene, remember that one of the women who followed Jesus and supported his ministry with her finances was Joanna, the wife of Herod Antipas's steward, a man named Chuza; see Lk 8:3.)

The story rings true with what we know of the characters: Antipas, the spineless, confused ruler, and Herodias, the power behind the throne, who is willing to go to any lengths to get her way. But why does Mark, who is so economical with his language, spend a full fifteen verses telling a story that has nothing to do with Jesus?

Three possible answers come to mind. First, the presence of such an extended story about John's death is consistent with the importance placed on him in all the Gospels. John's is the first voice we hear in Mark's Gospel. It is appropriate that we now hear the story of how that voice was silenced. Second, we place a great deal of emphasis on life situations in understanding the Scriptures in general and the life of Jesus in particular. The presence of this story affirms Mark's belief that we need to immerse ourselves in Jesus' life situation as well. He takes the time to help us understand Jesus' world.

A third reason seems even more compelling. Why would Mark spend precious time and space telling a story of someone who died at the hands of an irresponsible king? Because his readers are living in a similarly terrifying life situation. Their irresponsible king is Nero, and his modes of execution are far more grotesque than beheading. It is worth the time to tell the story of someone who sacrificed his life because of his faithfulness. Many of Mark's readers will be called to do the same.

PERFECT PROVISION

[30]The apostles gathered around Jesus and reported to Him all that they had done and taught. [31]He said to them, "Come away by yourselves to a remote place and rest a while." For many people were coming and going, and they did

not even have time to eat. ³²So they went away in the boat by themselves to a remote place, ³³but many saw them leaving and recognized them. People ran there by land from all the towns and arrived ahead of them. ³⁴So as He stepped ashore, He saw a huge crowd and had compassion on them, because they were like sheep without a shepherd. Then He began to teach them many things.

³⁵When it was already late, His disciples approached Him and said, "This place is a wilderness, and it is already late! ³⁶Send them away, so they can go into the surrounding countryside and villages to buy themselves something to eat."

³⁷"You give them something to eat," He responded.

They said to Him, "Should we go and buy 200 denarii worth of bread and give them something to eat?"

³⁸And He asked them, "How many loaves do you have? Go look."

When they found out they said, "Five, and two fish."

³⁹Then He instructed them to have all the people sit down in groups on the green grass. ⁴⁰So they sat down in ranks of hundreds and fifties. ⁴¹Then He took the five loaves and the two fish, and looking up to heaven, He blessed and broke the loaves. He kept giving them to His disciples to set before the people. He also divided the two fish among them all. ⁴²Everyone ate and was filled. ⁴³Then they picked up 12 baskets full of pieces of bread and fish. ⁴⁴Now those who ate the loaves were 5,000 men.

*T*he apostles, the "sent ones," now return from their sending and report back. They give Jesus an account of their work (which was, in reality, his work); they regale him with stories of their sowing of the Word (which was, in reality, his Word). Only Mark records the trying realities of the ministry—that Jesus was in fact trying to lead them to the wilderness to rest, that the Twelve were so caught up in the demands of ministry they did not have time to eat (see Mk 3:20).

All of the Gospels record the story of the feeding of the five thousand. The ever-present crowd follows the boat around the shoreline and waits for Jesus and the disciples to land on the other side. If you and I were exhausted and trying to get away for a period of rest, our response would most likely be frustration at finding a demanding mob waiting for us. Not so with Jesus. Mark, in tune with the range of his emotions, tells us that Jesus is deeply moved with compassion when he sees the crowd. Where we see an annoying mob with a bottomless need, Jesus sees a flock hungry for his Word. So he begins to teach. Once again, Mark leaves out the lesson!

We do not know how long the teaching lasts. Perhaps it is a series of shorter discussions; in any case, the day grows long. The disciples remind Jesus that they are in the wilderness and the crowd needs go to one of the surrounding villages to purchase food. Their statement echoes Moses' frustration when he cried out in the wilderness, "Where can I get meat to give all these people?" (Num 11:13). For Jesus, the wilderness is where extraordinary things occur. Though he earlier refused to make bread appear to feed himself in the wilderness (Mt 4:3-4), as an expression of the compassion he feels for his flock, the Shepherd exercises his authority and feeds them—in the wilderness.

Is there a twinkle in Jesus' eye when he gives the Twelve the impossible command "You give them something" (Mk 6:37)? Have they not just returned from a successful first mission? Jesus always calls upon his disciples to do the impossible: to forgive without limit, to love their enemies. His impossible commands force us to learn to depend totally on him. His call is always precisely to the level of our inadequacy.

Only the elderly John, who can remember details from sixty years ago with more clarity than what happened sixty minutes ago, will recall that they took the five loaves and two small fish from a nameless boy (Jn 6:9). In an image reminiscent of the Twenty-Third Psalm, Jesus orders the multitude to sit down in numbered groups on the "green grass" (a detail found only in Mark; see 6:39). The stage is set for a remarkable miracle.

But it will be an unmiraculous miracle. Jesus does with the loaves and fish what anyone of us might do at any other meal. He says the blessing. In his day, it would have sounded something like this:

Blessed art Thou, Eternal God our Father,
King of the Universe, who causes bread
to come forth from the earth.

The Mishnah, a collection of rabbinical teachings from 200 B.C. to A.D. 200, adds an additional blessing to be used if someone is in a place (like the wilderness) where a "miracle has been wrought":

Blessed is he that wrought miracles for our fathers in this place.

The miracle occurs in a matter of two verses. Yet Mark's language reflects nothing miraculous.[8] There is not a single murmur from the crowd. Does anyone present besides the disciples even know a miracle has occurred? Five thousand men (not to mention an additional ten thousand to fifteen thousand women and children) whom Jesus regards as sheep eat their fill on the green Galilee pasture—in the wilderness.

It is a remarkable, though apparently unrecognized, miracle. But there is often a miracle behind the miracle. That is what verse 43 is all about. In John 6:12, Jesus gives a very rabbinic command to pick up the pieces "so that nothing is wasted." In Judaism, food is sacred; it is the gift of God. Similarly, eating is sacred because it preserves life. It is an insult to God to waste the crumbs of food. So Jesus instructs the Twelve to canvass the vast area, probably several acres, and look among the blades of grass for the leftovers.[9] From the enormous field the Twelve recover only twelve small baskets of pieces. This is a miracle not of abundance, but of perfect provision.

The key to both miraculous feedings, of the four thousand and the five thousand, is in the specific Greek words used to describe the baskets. In every account of the feeding of the five thousand, the word used is *kofinos*. It indicates a small lunch-pail-sized basket. A different word is employed to describe the basket used in the feeding of the four thousand. It is *spyris*, which indicates a large "man-sized" basket, the type used to lower Paul over the wall in Acts 9:25. This detail is vital!

When Jesus recaps the two feeding miracles both in Mark 8:17-20 and Matthew 16:9-10, he uses these two distinct words to describe the baskets. The fact that the Gospels are consistent in this usage confirms the importance of this detail as we seek to understand the difference between the two events.

The miracle of the feeding of the five thousand is perfect provision.

The leftovers are meager, but they perfectly provide twelve lunch-sized baskets for the twelve disciples. It is a fulfillment of Jesus' own prayer to "give us today our daily bread" (Mt 6:11). It is an unmiraculous miracle, the same sort of miracle we often fail to recognize today when we receive our "daily bread." We celebrate abundant provision, but rarely are we equally amazed at the God who so intimately knows our needs that he provides perfectly—no more, no less than we need. When we take into account this intimacy, the miracle of perfect provision might well be the greater of the two.

Mark tells back to back the story of two banquets—one in a palace of unimaginable luxury, the other in a field of green grass. The focus of the first is the powerful king. The focus of the second is the hunger of the flock that is met by the miraculous provision of the servant-Shepherd.

THE INCOMPLETE STORY OF THE WATER WALKER

[45]Immediately He made His disciples get into the boat and go ahead of Him to the other side, to Bethsaida, while He dismissed the crowd. [46]After He said good-bye to them, He went away to the mountain to pray. [47]When evening came, the boat was in the middle of the sea, and He was alone on the land. [48]He saw them being battered as they rowed, because the wind was against them. Around three in the morning He came toward them walking on the sea and wanted to pass by them. [49]When they saw Him walking on the sea, they thought it was a ghost and cried out; [50]for they all saw Him and were terrified. Immediately He spoke with them and said, "Have courage! It is I. Don't be afraid." [51]Then He got into the boat with them, and the wind ceased. They were completely astounded, [52]because they had not understood about the loaves. Instead, their hearts were hardened.

[53]When they had crossed over, they came to land at Gennesaret and beached the boat. [54]As they got out of the boat, people immediately recognized Him. [55]They hurried throughout that vicinity and began to carry the sick on mats to wherever they heard He was. [56]Wherever He would go, into villages, towns, or the country, they laid the sick in the marketplaces and begged Him that they might touch just the tassel of His robe. And everyone who touched it was made well.

*J*esus does not linger in the afterglow of the perfect provision; instead he immediately compels the disciples to get into the boat to cut across the corner of the lake to the solitude of Bethsaida. He seems anxious to send them to wage their own war against the wind while he moves alone into the hills to pray.

From any one of the hills surrounding the lake you can look out and see a boat on any part of the lake. And if you have ever tried to row a boat into a strong wind, this story makes perfect sense. It is a desperate and hopeless task. Once again the disciples are working at the level of their own inadequacy.

The "fourth watch" (Mk 6:48 NIV) is Mark's Roman way of telling time. It represents the final of four watches of the night, from three to six a.m., the time when the sunrise begins to glow on the horizon. This incident should stand out clearly in our imaginations from the first storm in chapter 4. That was a demonic attack. This is a contrary wind. In the first story the boat almost sank; in this it is being blown in the opposite direction. In the first story Jesus is with the disciples, though he is asleep. In this story he is nowhere to be seen. Two separate storms on the Sea of Galilee, two separate miraculous feedings and two separate temple expulsions. We must get the flow of the ministry of Jesus clear in our minds and hearts.

In the early morning glow the exhausted disciples see a form coming across the water. His clothes and hair are being blown about by the strong wind. They watch in terror, long enough to see him come alongside and begin to pass by them in the direction they are so hopelessly rowing. Only one thing walks—or floats—on the water in the middle of the night: a ghost (*fantasma*). After Jesus calmed the storm in the first story in Mark 4, we are told the disciples were "terrified" by his power. Before, they were afraid because they saw a glimpse of who Jesus really was. Now they are terrified by not knowing it is Jesus. Sensing their fear, he cries out, "Take courage! It is I. Don't be afraid" (Mk 6:50). His words are literally "I am; no fear!"

When Moses asked to know God's name, the response was "I AM who I AM" (Ex 3:13). If God has a name, it is "I AM." He tells Moses in the same breath, "This is My name forever" (Ex 3:15). Standing on the waves amidst the blowing of the wind, Jesus identifies himself by that same name (see also Jn 10:30). Jesus comes closer, reaches up and grabs the gunwales, and hoists himself into the boat. The exhausting wind dies down.

Mark concludes the story with the key—the key to understanding just why the disciples do not recognize Jesus as the one walking on the water. Why? Because "they had not understood about the loaves" (Mk 6:52). But what hadn't they understood? Was the feeding so unmiraculous that they failed to recognize that providing bread (manna) in the wilderness was a characteristic of God? Just as walking on the water was something only God could do (Job 9:8)?

Mark's answer: their "hearts were hardened" (Mk 6:52). That is why they miss the miracles. That is why they fail to recognize the one who walks on the water. It is a characteristic they share with the Pharisees: stubborn disbelief. Even though they've received private instruction. Even though they've been out on their first successful mission. How could they have been so blind? How can we be so blind?

Before we leave the story of the water walker, I have one last question. What is missing in this story? What has Mark left out? If you don't know the answer, turn to Matthew 14:22-33. Mark, who records the personal remembrances of Peter, has left Peter out of the story. There is not a hint that anything uniquely involving Peter happened.

I used to believe the reason for the omission was Peter's pride. He did not want anyone reading of his "little faith" and the fact that he sank into the sea because of his disbelief. In time, after I came to know the mature rock of the book of Acts and his two letters, I have come to believe that Peter instructed Mark to leave him out of the story precisely because he did walk on the water. Humility is the reason for Peter's absence from the story, not pride. But there may be a better answer, and perhaps you can find it.

Though they were originally heading for Bethsaida, on the northern shore of the lake, they land instead at Gennesaret, on the western coast. They have been detoured by the wind. The ever-present crowd is there.

They have run from everywhere, bringing the sick for healing, placing them in front of Jesus as he tries to make his way through the marketplace. They beg and grasp and clutch his cloak, and the gracious Shepherd exudes the power to heal them all.

MARK 7

MORE UNORTHODOXY

7:1-23 Eating with unrinsed hands.

CRUMBS FOR THE PUPPIES

7:24-30 A pagan woman engages with Jesus.

AN UNSECRET HEALING

7:31-37 A prophetic healing.

MORE UNORTHODOXY

[1]*The Pharisees and some of the scribes who had come from Jerusalem gathered around Him.* [2]*They observed that some of His disciples were eating their bread with unclean—that is, unwashed—hands.* [3]*(For the Pharisees, in fact all the Jews, will not eat unless they wash their hands ritually, keeping the tradition of the elders.* [4]*When they come from the marketplace, they do not eat unless they have washed. And there are many other customs they have received and keep, like the washing of cups, jugs, copper utensils, and dining couches.)* [5]*Then the Pharisees and the scribes asked Him, "Why don't Your disciples live according to the tradition of the elders, instead of eating bread with ritually unclean hands?"*

[6]*He answered them, "Isaiah prophesied correctly about you hypocrites, as it is written:*

> *These people honor Me with their lips,*
> *but their heart is far from Me.*
> [7]*They worship Me in vain,*
> *teaching as doctrines the commands of men.*

[8]*Disregarding the command of God, you keep the tradition of men."* [9]*He also said to them, "You completely invalidate God's command in order to maintain your tradition!* [10]*For Moses said:*

> *Honor your father and your mother; and*
> *Whoever speaks evil of father or mother*
> *must be put to death.*

[11]*But you say, 'If a man tells his father or mother: Whatever benefit you might have received from me is Corban'" (that is, a gift [committed to the temple]),* [12]*"you no longer let him do anything for his father or mother.* [13]*You revoke God's word by your tradition that you have handed down. And you do many other similar things."* [14]*Summoning the crowd again, He told them, "Listen to Me, all of you, and understand:* [15]*Nothing that goes into a person from outside can defile him, but the things that come out of a person are what defile him.* [16]*If anyone has ears to hear, he should listen!"*

[17]*When He went into the house away from the crowd, the disciples asked Him about the parable.* [18]*And He said to them, "Are you also as lacking in un-*

derstanding? Don't you realize that nothing going into a man from the outside can defile him? [19]*For it doesn't go into his heart but into the stomach and is eliminated." (As a result, He made all foods clean.)* [20]*Then He said, "What comes out of a person—that defiles him.* [21]*For from within, out of people's hearts, come evil thoughts, sexual immoralities, thefts, murders,* [22]*adulteries, greed, evil actions, deceit, lewdness, stinginess, blasphemy, pride, and foolishness.* [23]*All these evil things come from within and defile a person."*

One of the ancient roads from Jerusalem north to Galilee winds through the plain of the Gennesaret and passes the shadow of Mount Arbel. It could be that an investigative committee from Jerusalem encountered Jesus and his disciples at the village of Gennesaret, which was close by that ancient road.

Until now the disciples have been observed breaking the oral law twice. They failed to fast (Mk 2:18) and they failed to observe the Sabbath (Mk 2:24). Jesus' men are now observed eating with "unclean" hands. We might translate the term "unrinsed" hands, for the Pharisees merely poured water over their hands. They did not literally wash them for practical cleanliness. Mark, in a parenthetical statement in verses 3 and 4, whispers this explanation to his Gentile Roman readers.

The question the Pharisees ask in Mark 7:5 is a frontal assault. The next seventeen verses are Jesus' extended answer to the question. The question literally opens with, "Why don't your disciples walk . . . ?" In Jesus' day, one of the Pharisees' principal categories for understanding the oral tradition was called *halachah*, which means "to walk." The image is of a devout person walking along a well-defined path of righteousness. To break the oral law or tradition was to depart from the "halachic" path of righteousness. Hence, Jesus' disciples were not walking according to the traditions.

One more piece of background helps us understand why the Pharisees accorded so much authority to the oral law, or "tradition." They revered the oral law because, according to their tradition, it was entrusted to Moses. An opening statement of a section of the Mishnah titled "The Fathers" reads:

Moses received the [oral] law from Sinai and committed it to Joshua, and Joshua to the elders, and the elders to the Prophets, and the Prophets committed it to the men of the great Synagogue. They said three things; be deliberate in judgment, raise many disciples and make a fence around the law. (Aboth 1:1-3)

The Pharisees gave their oral tradition as much authority as the written Torah because they believed it was given to Moses at the same time he was entrusted with the tablets of the law on Mount Sinai. When Moses came down from the mountain, he gave the law to Aaron and the priests and, according to the Pharisees, gave the oral law to Joshua and the elders. This established the Pharisees' claim that their authority came directly from Moses himself. They called themselves the "disciples of Moses" (see Jn 9:28). Jesus did not accept this tradition. With the prophet Isaiah, he looked upon the oral law as "the commands of men" (Mk 7:7).

Jesus opens his response by quoting Scripture. Isaiah describes the Pharisees perfectly as those who give God only lip service and vain worship. He then reveals the most glaring examples of their spiritually bankrupt traditions. The fifth commandment is "Honor your father and your mother" (Ex 20:12). The next chapter of Exodus outlines the penalty for breaking this command (Ex 21:17). Nothing could be clearer. But, says Jesus, the Pharisees have nullified the command of God by a tradition called "corban." The Hebrew word *qorban* literally means "offering" or "oblation." It appears eighty times in the Old Testament in the books of Leviticus, Numbers and Ezekiel. In its purest sense, it refers to an unblemished offering that reflects the love and consecration of the offerer (see 1 Pet 1:19).[10] It reflects God's command to offer sacrifice as an outer reflection of the inner reality of the heart.

But in Jesus' day the term had come to designate anything that was "consecrated to God," and in time it simply meant "forbidden," taking on the nuance of a curse. The Pharisees condoned the practice of declaring "corban" assets that should have been used by children to care for their parents. The asset need not have been given immediately to the temple, yet it was "forbidden" that it be used for any other purpose. It was considered "consecrated to God" though it remained in the use of the person who declared it "corban." In Jesus' mind, this practice nullified the command of God.

In Mark 7:14 Jesus turns to the crowd at large. His appeal is that they "listen" and "understand." (These words should be underlined. They will be lived out later in a chapter describing a prophetic healing.) Jesus is about to redefine the people's fundamental concepts of clean and unclean. Uncleanness, he says, comes from within, not from the outside. Rinsing your hands ceremonially has no effect whatsoever. He does not explain the statement to the crowd but leaves them to arrive at the "aha" moment on their own.

Later, in "the house" (Mk 7:17), Jesus' disciples refer to his statement as a parable, which strictly speaking it was not. Though "parable" can refer to any pregnant saying, the word implies something "thrown beside"—that is, it implies that "this is like that" (e.g., "The kingdom is like a seed"). Jesus' statement was straightforward. Its implications were simply beyond any of the disciples.

Things from the outside don't enter the heart; they go into the stomach and eventually out the body. Mark interrupts Jesus here with an earth-shattering parenthetical comment: "As a result, He made all foods clean" (Mk 7:19). Remember when Peter experienced the vision in Acts 10:9-16—and repeated it almost word for word again in Acts 11:2-18? He was told in the dream to "kill and eat" an array of unclean animals. In remembering the words of Jesus, Peter's rooftop vision became more focused. Only Mark's Gospel records these words.

Jesus continues, "From within, out of people's hearts, come evil thoughts" (Mk 7:21). He might have said that uncleanness resides in the imagination. Every one of the sins in Jesus' list begins in the imagination. Evil renders one unclean, not eating with unrinsed hands or touching a corpse or being overshadowed by a leper. Nonconformity to an oral tradition is no longer sin. This is a world turned upside down.

CRUMBS FOR THE PUPPIES

24He got up and departed from there to the region of Tyre and Sidon. He entered a house and did not want anyone to know it, but He could not escape notice. 25Instead, immediately after hearing about Him, a woman whose

little daughter had an unclean spirit came and fell at His feet. ²⁶Now the woman was Greek, a Syrophoenician by birth, and she kept asking Him to drive the demon out of her daughter. ²⁷He said to her, "Allow the children to be satisfied first, because it isn't right to take the children's bread and throw it to the dogs."

²⁸But she replied to Him, "Lord, even the dogs under the table eat the children's crumbs."

²⁹Then He told her, "Because of this reply, you may go. The demon has gone out of your daughter." ³⁰When she went back to her home, she found her child lying on the bed, and the demon was gone.

The story of the Syrophoenician woman is a fascinating echo of an earlier story of the faith of the centurion. Both are "long-distance" miracles. Both involve the faith of a Gentile. Jesus has fled the draining presence of the crowd in an effort to get some rest. Again he discovers that this is impossible. A desperate woman invades the silence that surrounds him. Perhaps she has heard of his power from her countrymen who saw him earlier (Mk 3:8). She frantically falls at his feet, begging for a miracle.

Rabbis were not supposed to speak to any women in public, much less Gentile women. But Jesus engages this worried woman in an unforgettable conversation. At first his response sounds like a refusal. In fact it is an invitation to lean in to his heart.

Jesus' reply sounds harsh. Is he really calling her a dog? Dogs were unclean animals in Judaism (Lev 11:27). But Jesus does not use the common word for stray dogs. He uses the diminutive term for "little dogs" or perhaps "pet dogs." The scene he is painting for the woman is not a Jewish scene but a Gentile one. In her world it was common to keep small pet dogs. The image of the children throwing scraps of bread to their pets underneath the table does not offend her in the least. In fact, it has the opposite effect. Her charming but stubborn response delights Jesus. It represents an imaginative expression of her faith in Jesus. In the give-and-take of ordinary human conversation, Jesus is enchanted by the faith and wit of this extraordinary woman.

When she returns home, the dark demonic cloud is gone. Her little girl is lying quietly in bed—no more convulsions, no more self-destructive behavior. Her home and her family will never be the same, and all of this represents just a crumb fallen from the table!

But, once again, the long-distance healing of the little girl is not the point of the story. There is always a miracle behind the miracle. In this exchange it is the persistent faith of the Gentile woman that is miraculous. Without realizing it she has asked for something she does not deserve. She has asked for mercy.

AN UNSECRET HEALING

[31] Again, leaving the region of Tyre, He went by way of Sidon to the Sea of Galilee, through the region of the Decapolis. [32] They brought to Him a deaf man who also had a speech difficulty, and begged Jesus to lay His hand on him. [33] So He took him away from the crowd privately. After putting His fingers in the man's ears and spitting, He touched his tongue. [34] Then, looking up to heaven, He sighed deeply and said to him, "Ephphatha!" (that is, "Be opened!"). [35] Immediately his ears were opened, his speech difficulty was removed, and he began to speak clearly. [36] Then He ordered them to tell no one, but the more He would order them, the more they would proclaim it.

[37] They were extremely astonished and said, "He has done everything well! He even makes deaf people hear, and people unable to speak, talk!"

*I*f your Bible has maps in the back, turn to a map of Israel and trace the circuitous route of Jesus in Mark 7:31. He travels some twenty miles north to the city of Sidon, a pagan town. He then turns southeast forty miles back to the shore of the Lake of Galilee. He moves along the shore, due south, back to the area of the Decapolis. This route seems intended to keep him outside of Galilee.

When he arrives in an undisclosed area of the Decapolis, he is met by a group of people who have heard of his healing power—probably from the preaching of the Gadarene demoniac. Even though Jesus is in an area dominated by paganism, this crowd appears to be Jewish. His command to keep the matter is secret (Mark 7:36) is one indication.

That charge has only been issued to Jews in Mark's Gospel. The second reason to assume they might be Jewish is the method of Jesus' healing. The opening of this man's ears is told only by Mark. The way Jesus goes about the healing is "prophetic activity"—it becomes a parable for the opening of the spiritual ears of Jesus' followers (see Mark 7:14, 18). (We will witness another healing with the same prophetic character in Mark 8:22-26. These miracles occur only in the Gospel of Mark.)

Jesus places his fingers in the man's ears, reminiscent of Isaiah 35:5. He spits and touches the man's tongue, echoing Isaiah 35:6. Mark's term for Jesus' "deep sigh" or "groan" is related to the same word Paul uses for the Spirit's groaning on our behalf in Romans 8:26. This is the emotional Jesus. From the depths of that deep sigh comes the Aramaic word *Ephphatha*. We are privileged to hear Jesus' voice in his own tongue.

Despite Jesus' command that everyone keep it secret, word of the miracle spreads. As a result, in Mark 8:1, Jesus will face another crowd of thousands of hungry people. The nameless man who can now hear and speak plainly represents a living parable for Mark. His healing has been prophetic. Jesus' groaning words, "Be opened," represent the deepest hope of the gospel: that you and I might truly hear and eventually clearly speak the good news.

MARK 8

ANOTHER FEAST, A DIFFERENT MIRACLE

8:1-13 The feeding of the four thousand.

ANOTHER MISUNDERSTANDING ABOUT BREAD

8:14-21 The "yeast" of Herod and the Pharisees.

EYES PROGRESSIVELY OPENED

8:22-26 Another prophetic healing.

MORE THAN HE KNOWS

8:27-30 Peter's confession.

WHAT "MESSIAH" MEANS

8:31-38 Jesus predicts his death.

ANOTHER FEAST, A DIFFERENT MIRACLE

¹In those days there was again a large crowd, and they had nothing to eat. He summoned the disciples and said to them, ²"I have compassion on the crowd, because they've already stayed with Me three days and have nothing to eat. ³If I send them home famished, they will collapse on the way, and some of them have come a long distance."

⁴His disciples answered Him, "Where can anyone get enough bread here in this desolate place to fill these people?"

⁵"How many loaves do you have?" He asked them.

"Seven," they said. ⁶Then He commanded the crowd to sit down on the ground. Taking the seven loaves, He gave thanks, broke the [loaves], and kept on giving [them] to His disciples to set before [the people]. So they served the [loaves] to the crowd. ⁷They also had a few small fish, and when He had blessed them, He said these were to be served as well. ⁸They ate and were filled. Then they collected seven large baskets of leftover pieces. ⁹About 4,000 [men] were there. He dismissed them ¹⁰and immediately got into the boat with His disciples and went to the district of Dalmanutha.

¹¹The Pharisees came out and began to argue with Him, demanding of Him a sign from heaven to test Him. ¹²But sighing deeply in His spirit, He said, "Why does this generation demand a sign? I assure you: No sign will be given to this generation!" ¹³Then He left them, got on board [the boat] again, and went to the other side.

𝓙esus, still in the area of the Decapolis (Mk 7:31), has spent three days teaching in the open air. The crowd is a mix of Gentiles and Jews. Mark tells the story of the second miraculous feeding in strict parallel with the first.[11] Scholars who claim only one feeding miracle occurred base their position on the presupposition that the Gospel writers confused one story for two. But we have two distinct stories, two different locations, two different crowds and, most especially, two completely different miraculous outcomes.

Having spent three days with this crowd, Jesus finds it unthinkable to send them away hungry. The disciples seem to have forgotten the

feeding of the five thousand. They protested then that the cost of buying food for so many was prohibitive if not impossible (Mk 6:37). Now
they complain that the location is too remote. Earlier Mark mentioned
they did not understand about the bread because of the hardness of
their hearts (Mk 6:52).

Beginning with the feeding of the five thousand, Mark's narrative has been tied together by bread as an underlying theme. The
multitude was provided with miraculous bread (Mk 6:30). The
Pharisees were concerned that the disciples were eating bread with
unwashed hands (Mk 7:2). The Gentile woman asked for the crumbs
of bread that fell from the table (Mk 7:28). Now the four thousand
will be fed by the multiplication of the seven loaves of bread (Mk
8:1-7). Later Jesus will have a heated discussion with the Twelve
concerning bread (Mk 8:16). In Mark 8:4 the disciples whine,
"Where can anyone get enough bread?"

At the earlier feeding of the five thousand, Jesus engaged his disciples with the impossible command "You give them something to eat"
(Mk 6:37). Now he seems to lack the energy to engage them. "How
many loaves do you have?" he simply asks (Mk 8:5).

As before (Mk 6:39), the crowd is instructed to sit. There is no mention of the green grass of Galilee. As before, the miracle is virtually
undetectable in terms of Mark's language. Jesus pronounces a blessing,
breaks the loaves and passes them to the disciples. He does the same
with a few small fish. There is no hint of amazement. The thousands
simply eat and are satisfied. You begin to wonder if Mark's purpose is
to underwhelm. Are we left to be overwhelmed by the lack of spiritual
perception on the part of the Twelve?

Again in parallel form to the earlier story, the leftover pieces are
gathered. All that is different is the Greek word for "basket." Here, as
in Matthew 15:37, the word used is *spyris*, a man-sized hamper or basket. It is the word used of the basket in which Paul was lowered in Acts
9:25. There are seven extremely large baskets of leftovers when initially
there were only seven small loaves of bread. The miracle is clearly one
of abundance. These are significant distinctions that need to be woven
into our understanding of the flow of the ministry of Jesus.

Dismissing the crowd, Jesus and the disciples get into the boat once more and depart for a region referred to as Dalmanutha. Scholars have been unable to positively identify its location. Matthew, telling the same story, refers to it as the region of Magadan, or Magdala, which lies on the western shore of the lake, close to Gennesaret, where the boat had blown ashore after the second windstorm (Mk 6:53).

The consistent image we encounter is that of Jesus and the Twelve crisscrossing the lake from east to west in order to avoid the ever-increasing crowd. The Galilean ministry is now over. Jesus will return to this area only in secret (Mk 9:30).

When they arrive in Dalmanutha, the Pharisees are waiting. Their strategy has shifted. No longer are they on the lookout for Sabbath violations. Now, for the first and only time in Mark, they demand that Jesus gave them a sign. The nuance of the word "signs" (*semeion*) in the Synoptic Gospels is negative. In Matthew, Mark and Luke, signs are demanded of Jesus by people who refuse to believe. To demand a sign reveals a precondition of stubborn disbelief. People who demand signs never believe them when they come. In John's Gospel a sign has a more positive connotation. It is something given by God.

Jesus' emotional response reveals all. He sighs "deeply in His spirit," Mark says. No sign will be given, Jesus says as he turns and departs once more for the other side of the lake.

ANOTHER MISUNDERSTANDING ABOUT BREAD

[14]They had forgotten to take bread and had only one loaf with them in the boat. [15]Then He commanded them: "Watch out! Beware of the yeast of the Pharisees and the yeast of Herod."

[16]They were discussing among themselves that they did not have any bread. [17]Aware of this, He said to them, "Why are you discussing that you do not have any bread? Do you not yet understand or comprehend? Is your heart hardened? [18]Do you have eyes, and not see, and do you have ears, and not hear? And do you not remember? [19]When I broke the five loaves for the 5,000, how many baskets full of pieces of bread did you collect?"

"Twelve," they told Him.

20 "When I broke the seven loaves for the 4,000, how many large baskets full of pieces of bread did you collect?"

"Seven," they said.

21 And He said to them, "Don't you understand yet?"

*I*n Mark 8:11-21, the dual themes of bread and misunderstanding continue. As the disciples cross to the other side of the lake, Jesus uses the rare uncrowded moment to teach in private. He warns them against the yeast of the Pharisees and Herod. The two share one common characteristic: they both ask for signs (see Lk 23:8). Yeast is an image common in Judaism. The disciples should have understood. It represents, on one hand, something small that in time can have a large effect. Jesus employs the image in Matthew 13:31-33 in parallel with that of the small mustard seed, which yields a large plant. The other nuance of the term "yeast" has to do with corruption or evil. Paul's writings reflect the idea of yeast as a bad influence. Though small in the beginning, it has a devastating effect on the community (1 Cor 5:6-8; Gal 5:9).

In Mark 8:16 the confusion of the Twelve centers on bread. A sense of urgency begins at this point in the narrative as we sense Jesus' growing frustration. The ministry is rapidly coming to a close. The Twelve are still hopelessly lacking in spiritual understanding. We can hear the vexation in Jesus' voice in Mark 8:17. Listen to his words, the layers of questions. Do they not see or understand? Are their hearts hardened? Though they have eyes and ears, they fail to see and hear. Jesus' questions provide the key to understanding the two healings in this chapter. In the first, of someone who had ears but was deaf, Jesus heals with the exclamation "Be opened!" (Mk 8:32-35). The second prophetic healing will come when Jesus progressively opens the eyes of the blind man in Mark 8:22-26.

Jesus recaps the results of the two feedings. He uses the two different Greek words to describe the baskets involved in each separate event.

"Don't you remember?" He presses them. They seem to clearly remember the numbers, the twelve lunch pails and the seven hampers full of leftovers. He leaves the disciples with a poignant, unanswered question: "Don't you understand yet?" (Mk 8:21; see also Mk 4:13, 33; 7:14; 8:32-33; 14:68).

What is it the disciples don't understand? They have witnessed Jesus' power to provide both perfect and abundant provision. It is pointless for them to argue about forgetting to bring bread along for the voyage. But they still seem to be blind to Jesus' true identity and power. They are either oblivious or afraid.

In a deeper sense, they are deaf to the urgency of the moment. Jesus warns them of the danger of creeping stubbornness and disbelief, of the effect it can have, blinding and deafening them. This seems to be a preparation for the ultimate revelation that he is the bread of perfect and abundant provision. That costly realization, though it is closing in on them fast, seems a world away.

EYES PROGRESSIVELY OPENED

22 Then they came to Bethsaida. They brought a blind man to Him and begged Him to touch him. 23 He took the blind man by the hand and brought him out of the village. Spitting on his eyes and laying His hands on him, He asked him, "Do you see anything?"

24 He looked up and said, "I see people—they look to me like trees walking."

25 Again Jesus placed His hands on the man's eyes, and he saw distinctly. He was cured and could see everything clearly. 26 Then He sent him home, saying, "Don't even go into the village."

*F*rom Magadan the disciples flee the Pharisees, crossing back once more to the familiarity of Peter's original hometown of Bethsaida, a village considerably larger even than Capernaum. It was completely destroyed by an earthquake in A.D. 115 and was never re-inhabited.

The healing of the blind man is more than a miracle. It is a parable and a prophecy of the gradual but inevitable opening of Peter's and all the disciples' eyes. Paralleling the first prophetic healing of the deaf man in Mark 7:33, Jesus takes the nameless man and leads him to a private place. The use of spit in the healing is a mystery. In John 9:6

Jesus uses his spit to make mud. He does this in order to deliberately violate the oral law regarding work on the Sabbath—there was a specific law against spitting. But here there is no mention of the Sabbath.

What is without precedence is the appearance of failure. When Jesus asks if the man can see anything, he responds that the people look like trees—that is, they seem shapeless and out of focus. Jesus places his hands on his eyes a second time and the cure is complete. As in the previous prophetic healing, he is commanded to keep clear of the village, to keep the miracle a secret as long as possible.

Mark, as he will continue to do to the very end of his Gospel, leaves us hanging. As with Jesus' parables, we are left with the story, in sovereign freedom to engage or not. The "aha" moment is waiting for those who will listen and hear and look and see. For the moment, maybe we see the spiritual world out of focus. Jesus promises us the hope of clear spiritual perception.

This is a variation of Mark's bookend device. The bookends are the two unique healings: one of a deaf man, the other of someone who is blind. Between the bookends is an extended exposé of the failure of the disciples to hear or see. Until this moment, they have seen Jesus as shapeless and out of focus. That is all about to radically change.

MORE THAN HE KNOWS

27Jesus went out with His disciples to the villages of Caesarea Philippi. And on the road He asked His disciples, "Who do people say that I am?"

28They answered Him, "John the Baptist; others, Elijah; still others, one of the prophets."

29 "But you," He asked them again, "who do you say that I am?"

Peter answered Him, "You are the Messiah!"

*F*rom Bethsaida the disciples strike out north to the area of Caesarea Philippi, twenty-five miles distant. This was Antipas's brother Philip's capital city, hence named Philippi. And it could not have been more different than the village they'd left behind. Caesarea was a thoroughly pagan area. Herod the Great had constructed a temple for the worship of his patron, the deified Augustus. Next to this temple was the cave of Pan and its temple. Pan was a mythological creature, a satyr with the legs of a goat and the body of the man. He was worshiped as a god of shepherds and mountains. In time there would be a temple to Zeus in the same complex.

It is as if Jesus intends to lead the Twelve into the heart of paganism to ask them this supremely important question. Amidst temples where an emperor and even a goat are revered as gods and worshiped, Jesus asks, "Who do people say that I am?" (Mk 8:29). It is the moment toward which the first half of Mark's Gospel has been building. Their initial answer is nothing new. We heard this list before in Mark 6:14. The rumors have centered on John or perhaps Elijah or one of the other prophets.

Listen carefully to Jesus' second question. It is deliberately pointed and focused. "But you . . . who do you say I am?" (Mk 8:29). All at once Peter seems to be the only other person on stage. He does not precisely answer the question as it was originally worded. That is, he does not respond, "We say you are . . . " Peter speaks with a confidence and certainty that come from beyond himself. He says more than he knows, as his eyes gradually begin to see: "You are the Messiah" (Mk 8:29).

Most likely at Peter's insistence, Mark leaves out the wonderful blessing Jesus speaks over Peter after his confession, proclaiming that he has finally earned the name "the rock" (Mt 16:18). It is a title Peter will never claim exclusively for himself but share with the entire church (1 Pet 2:5).

The ominous, luminous words have finally been spoken. They fulfill part one of Mark 1:1—Jesus is the Christ. Now he strictly warns them to say nothing of it for now, because Jesus must teach them what "Messiah" truly means.

WHAT "MESSIAH" MEANS

30 And He strictly warned them to tell no one about Him.

31 Then He began to teach them that the Son of Man must suffer many things and be rejected by the elders, the chief priests, and the scribes, be killed, and rise after three days. 32 He was openly talking about this. So Peter took Him aside and began to rebuke Him.

33But turning around and looking at His disciples, He rebuked Peter and said, "Get behind Me, Satan, because you're not thinking about God's concerns, but man's!"

34Summoning the crowd along with His disciples, He said to them, "If anyone wants to be My follower, he must deny himself, take up his cross, and follow Me. 35For whoever wants to save his life will lose it, but whoever loses his life because of Me and the gospel will save it. 36For what does it benefit a man to gain the whole world yet lose his life? 37What can a man give in exchange for his life? 38For whoever is ashamed of Me and of My words in this adulterous and sinful generation, the Son of Man will also be ashamed of him when He comes in the glory of His Father with the holy angels."

The fateful word "Messiah" has been spoken for the first time in Mark's Gospel. Amidst a swirl of misunderstandings concerning the "anointed one," Jesus sets out to undeceive the Twelve. At the time, "Messiah" represented a wide range of hopes and dreams in Israel. To some he would be a glorious king who, with Jerusalem as his throne, would reestablish the theocratic nation of Israel. To many he would be a militaristic Messiah who would come and kill the Roman oppressor. What these differing dreams all held in common was the notion of glory, victory and divine power. Above all, the Messiah would never submit, surrender or suffer.

But in Mark 8:31, Jesus begins the painful process of redefining and undeceiving the disciples. The Son of Man, Jesus tells them, will suffer, be rejected and finally be killed. With the emotional shock of those words, the disciples all stop listening. It is too much for them to process. As often as he will repeat himself concerning his suffering and death, they do not really hear the words "and rise after three days" (Mk 8:31).

Peter takes Jesus aside and rebukes him for this foolishness. Matthew tells us he said, "This will never happen to You!" (Mt 16:22). Peter convinced Mark to omit the earlier blessing, but Mark does not forget to record Jesus' curse. If you look closely at the wording, you will see that the previous blessing has been turned on its head. Jesus blessed Peter, saying his words had not come from man but from the Father (Mt 16:17). But after Peter's denial of this disturbing new definition of Messiah, the blessing becomes a curse: "Get behind me, Satan; you are not thinking the things of God but the things of men" (Mk 8:33, author's translation). Jesus had warned them that Satan would try to come and steal the Word that had been sown in their hearts (Mk 4:15).

The gruesome details of Mark 8:31 seem to have been spoken privately to the Twelve. Now Jesus summons the ever-present crowd of followers. The lesson shifts dramatically. At first Jesus told the Twelve what it would cost him to be the Messiah. Now he tells the crowd at large what it will cost them to follow the Messiah. It is the first of three such pronouncements (see also Mk 9:31; 10:33). His cross will lead to their crosses. The loss of his life will lead to their lives being offered up for him and the gospel. He is going to turn the world upside down in ways we still struggle to understand. We will save our lives by losing them. The surpassing value of a single soul Jesus places above the worth of the whole world.

MARK 9

REVELATION AND FEAR

9:1–13 The transfiguration.

BELIEVING AND NOT BELIEVING

9:14–32 The healing of a boy with a demon.

A RECURRING ARGUMENT

9:33–37 The disciples ask who is greatest.

SALTED WITH FIRE

9:38–50 The flavor of the little ones.

REVELATION AND FEAR

[1]*Then He said to them, "I assure you: There are some standing here who will not taste death until they see the kingdom of God come in power."*

[2]*After six days Jesus took Peter, James, and John and led them up on a high mountain by themselves to be alone. He was transformed in front of them,* [3]*and His clothes became dazzling—extremely white as no launderer on earth could whiten them.* [4]*Elijah appeared to them with Moses, and they were talking with Jesus.*

[5]*Then Peter said to Jesus, "Rabbi, it's good for us to be here! Let us make three tabernacles: one for You, one for Moses, and one for Elijah"—*[6]*because he did not know what he should say, since they were terrified.*

[7]*A cloud appeared, overshadowing them, and a voice came from the cloud:*

This is My beloved Son;
listen to Him!

[8]*Then suddenly, looking around, they no longer saw anyone with them except Jesus alone.*

[9]*As they were coming down from the mountain, He ordered them to tell no one what they had seen until the Son of Man had risen from the dead.* [10]*They kept this word to themselves, discussing what "rising from the dead" meant.*

[11]*Then they began to question Him, "Why do the scribes say that Elijah must come first?"*

[12]*"Elijah does come first and restores everything," He replied. "How then is it written about the Son of Man that He must suffer many things and be treated with contempt?* [13]*But I tell you that Elijah really has come, and they did to him whatever they wanted, just as it is written about him."*

Chapter divisions in the Gospels were a later addition to the text and sometimes occur in places that break up the flow of the narrative. Some scholars, such as Gordon Fee, believe we should do away with them altogether. The division between Mark 8 and 9 comes at an unfortunate place. It breaks a single statement Jesus made into two parts. In Mark 8:38, Jesus has been speaking of coming "in the glory of his Father," a reference to the end times. The second half of that same train of thought occurs in Mark 9:1, hence the unfortunate break.

In the Greek text, verse 1 begins with "and" (*kai*), though we might translate it as "but." "But he said to them, 'I assure you: There are some standing here who will not taste death until they see the kingdom of God come in power'" (Mk 9:1). This is the statement all the Gospels use to introduce the story of the transfiguration. In light of the fact that Jesus will return in the Father's glory on the day of his coming, he will reveal that glory to these three disciples before they taste death. Of all Peter experienced with Jesus, the transfiguration is the only event he refers to in his writings. He understood that he had witnessed a picture of the coming kingdom:

> For when He received honor and glory from God the Father, a voice came to Him from the Majestic Glory:
>
> > This is My beloved Son.
> > I take delight in Him!
>
> And we heard this voice when it came from heaven while we were with Him on the holy mountain. (2 Pet 1:17-18)

It is absolutely vital to understand that the transfiguration took place after Peter's confession. It was not proof of Jesus' identity. Peter and the others had begun to grasp the truth the only way it can be grasped: by faith.

After the four have made their way up the unidentified mountain, we are told with typical Markan abruptness that Jesus was "transfigured" (*metamorphoō*). Paul uses the same word twice in his writings to describe the process by which the Holy Spirit works in us to transform and renew our minds (Rom 12:2; 2 Cor 3:18). Strictly speaking, Jesus is not transformed but transfigured. A veil is momentarily lifted and the three disciples see who Jesus has been all along. It is a continuation of the progressive opening of their eyes.

Peter's somewhat homespun description, that Jesus' clothes appeared whiter than any launderer could wash them, appears only in Mark's account. With Jesus in the brilliant light appear Moses and Elijah, the only two prophets who ascended Sinai and met with God (Ex 19:1-3; 1 Kings 19:8-18—Sinai is referred to as "Horeb" in the 1 Kings passage). The two patriarchs represent the Law and the Prophets. They represent all those who have suffered because of their obedience to the Father. They represent the two categories of citizens of the kingdom of God: those who die and those who will be taken up before they die. Moses and Elijah are talking with Jesus. Only Luke hints at the content of their conversation. He says they are talking about Jesus' death (Lk 9:31).

Only Peter speaks. This account is his remembrance. In order to best understand this moment we must remember the context. Mark says the disciples are terrified. Panic is behind each of Peter's confused words. His first statement is better understood as a question: "Rabbi, is it good for us to be here?" As far as Peter is concerned, it is not a good thing for him to be there. If this radiance is the light of God's glory, he thinks he is about to taste the death Jesus has spoken of in Mark 9:1 (see Ex 33:20). Perhaps he thinks this is the final coming itself.

Engage with your imagination for a moment. Here is an observant Jewish man facing Moses and Elijah, bathed in a radiant light that all his life he has been told will kill him. Perhaps he is dying. Perhaps the kingdom is breaking in at that very moment! The parenthetical statement in Mark 9:6, that Peter did not know what to say, is a sure indicator that what he does eventually say will be the wrong thing.

Peter asks if they might erect three "tabernacles" (Mk 9:5). The Greek word, which appears in all three accounts of the transfiguration, is *skēnē*. It simply means "tent" and is sometimes translated as "shelter." Might Peter in his moment of terror have been asking to build tents for the three luminous characters in order that he and his companions be "sheltered" from their potentially lethal light? It does not make perfect sense, but Peter confesses that he might not have been making perfect sense at the moment. The context is Sinai, terror, impending doom and radiant splendor.

Peter needn't have worried about shelter. At that moment God shelters them all with a cloud, and the same voice that echoed at Sinai speaks the words both Peter and Jesus need to hear. The progressive opening of Peter's eyes and ears leaps ahead light years as God's voice identifies Jesus as his "beloved Son." Then God, perhaps as frustrated with the disciples as Jesus has been, urges, "Listen to him!" (Mk 9:7).

The "suddenly" of verse 8 is not Mark's well-worn *eutheos*. It is a word that appears only once in the New Testament: *exapina*. It denotes something unexpected. When the disciples look up, what they see is not what they expected to see: Jesus alone and once more . . . ordinary.

Later, when Peter witnesses the crucifixion from afar, all he will see is a man on a cross. After the resurrection, Jesus, though he can pass through locked doors, will appear to be normal. When in Acts 1:9 he is "taken up," there is no language of illumination. It is the Jesus the disciples have always known, hidden by another cloud. The transfiguration is the only occasion when they witness his true radiant glory. On their way back down the mountain, Jesus issues his usual order for them to keep silent, but for the first time he adds, "until the Son of Man [has] risen from the dead" (Mk 9:9).

For once they obey Jesus' gag order. The disciples keep this experience to themselves but discuss what "rising from the dead" might mean. Surely, they reason, it cannot literally mean "rising from the dead"!

If we are not careful, we might read right over Mark 9:11-13. These verses represent a subtle but significant shift for the disciples. Simply put, the disciples begin to ask better questions. Having just seen Elijah, they wonder why he has apparently come second (i.e., after Jesus) when Malachi 4:5 says Elijah will come first. It is a good question, and Jesus answers it apparently with none of his usual frustration. Elijah has come first, he says, referring to his cousin John (see Mt 11:14; 17:12). They did to him what it pleased them to do. They murdered him.

Every bit the rabbi, Jesus responds to their question with another, better question: Why do the Scriptures say the Son of Man must suffer and be treated with contempt? Take note of the progression. Jesus introduced them to the fact of his upcoming suffering just after Peter's confession in Mark 8:31-32. He repeated the note of suffering as they descended the Mount of Transfiguration. Now he challenges them to a biblical understanding of that suffering. He challenges you and me to develop the same understanding of the redemptive nature of his suffering and ours.

BELIEVING AND NOT BELIEVING

14When they came to the disciples, they saw a large crowd around them and scribes disputing with them. 15All of a sudden, when the whole crowd saw Him, they were amazed and ran to greet Him. 16Then He asked them, "What are you arguing with them about?"

17Out of the crowd, one man answered Him, "Teacher, I brought my son to You. He has a spirit that makes him unable to speak. 18Wherever it seizes him, it throws him down, and he foams at the mouth, grinds his teeth, and becomes rigid. So I asked Your disciples to drive it out, but they couldn't."

19He replied to them, "You unbelieving generation! How long will I be with you? How long must I put up with you? Bring him to Me." 20So they brought him to Him. When the spirit saw Him, it immediately convulsed the boy. He fell to the ground and rolled around, foaming at the mouth. 21"How long has this been happening to him?" Jesus asked his father.

"From childhood," he said. 22"And many times it has thrown him into fire or water to destroy him. But if You can do anything, have compassion on us and help us."

23Then Jesus said to him, "'If You can?' Everything is possible to the one who believes."

24Immediately the father of the boy cried out, "I do believe! Help my unbelief."

25When Jesus saw that a crowd was rapidly coming together, He rebuked the unclean spirit, saying to it, "You mute and deaf spirit, I command you: come out of him and never enter him again!"

26Then it came out, shrieking and convulsing him violently. The boy became like a corpse, so that many said, "He's dead." 27But Jesus, taking him by the hand, raised him, and he stood up.

28After He went into a house, His disciples asked Him privately, "Why couldn't we drive it out?"

29And He told them, "This kind can come out by nothing but prayer [and fasting]."

30Then they left that place and made their way through Galilee, but He did not want anyone to know it. 31For He was teaching His disciples and telling them, "The Son of Man is being betrayed into the hands of men. They will kill Him, and after He is killed, He will rise three days later." [32]*But they did not understand this statement, and they were afraid to ask Him.*

*T*he crowd is always waiting, after each crossing of the lake and now as they descend from the mountaintop experience with Moses and Elijah. The moment they recognize Jesus, they run to him in amazement. There has been an argument with a group of scribes at the foot of the mountain, but Mark never tells us what the argument was about. The apparent answer comes from a frustrated and frightened father. He has brought his demon-possessed son to Jesus for healing. Discovering that he was not there but on the mountain, he begged the disciples to exorcise the demon. They failed.

In Mark 9:19, we see Jesus at one of his most emotional moments in this Gospel. If we are to understand these feelings, we need to take into account where Jesus has just been. I wonder if, for those few luminous moments on the mountain, Jesus felt the tremendous weight of his human experience mercifully lifted for a time. What greater encouragement than fellowship with Moses and Elijah and hearing the voice of his Father declaring his love? On the way down the mountain, he has experienced a substantial and engaging discussion after the three disciples' better question. After these satisfying moments, Jesus appears on the scene only to hear bickering and to witness the failure of his disciples to do something they were able to do earlier, on their first mission trip. As we will see in the verses that follow, the deep source of his frustration is their unbelief.

As the boy is brought, the demon throws him into a final convulsion in one last attempt to destroy him. The father's response to Jesus' question affirms this; from childhood it has been trying to kill him. The father has no idea what buttons he is pushing in Jesus when he asks, "If You can do anything . . . " (Mk 9:22). I imagine Jesus turning from the boy writhing on the ground and facing the father squarely. *"If* you can?" he responds. The pressure of the situation leads to new clarity. The father blurts out, "I do believe! Help my unbelief" (Mk 9:24). As contradictory as these words might seem, the pressure of the life-and-death situation brings into focus deep truths. In the tangle of the human heart we sometimes do believe and disbelieve in the same moment. That is, until something or someone appears to help us with our unbelief.

The ever-present crowd is running to the scene. Jesus senses that he has only a few seconds to do what needs to be done. He issues the authoritative command and the demon has no choice but to obey. Perhaps the demon does finally kill the boy in the process and those who think he is dead are right. Nevertheless, Jesus takes the boy's hand and raises him up.

Afterward, they enter a house of undisclosed location. In a private moment the embarrassed disciples ask why they failed. Jesus, implying that there are different kinds of demons, says this particular kind is only overcome by prayer. To pray is to totally give the situation over to God, allowing his power to redeem the situation. The disciples were trying to cast out the demon in their own power. Instead, they need to learn to completely depend on God's power working through them. Jesus confesses that even he can do nothing without the Father.

As they secretly pass through Galilee on their way back to Capernaum, Jesus spends more focused time instructing the disciples. He presses the point. He is going to be killed but raised to life on the third day. In a priceless insight, Mark tells us the disciples still do not understand. Most significantly, "They were afraid to ask Him" (Mk 9:32).

A RECURRING ARGUMENT

33 Then they came to Capernaum. When He was in the house, He asked them, "What were you arguing about on the way?" 34 But they were silent, because on the way they had been arguing with one another about who was the greatest. 35 Sitting down, He called the Twelve and said to them, "If anyone wants to be first, he must be last of all and servant of all." 36 Then He took a child, had him stand among them, and taking him in His arms, He said to them, 37 "Whoever welcomes one little child such as this in My name welcomes Me. And whoever welcomes Me does not welcome Me, but Him who sent Me."

*F*or the last time the disciples and Jesus return to the familiarity of the home base in Capernaum. It is Peter's house they enter. Jesus has overheard them arguing on the road. He asks what it was all about. The disciples, embarrassed and perhaps afraid to bring the issue to light, won't reveal that they have been arguing about which one of them is the greatest. It is an argument that will surface again and again as they make their way to Jerusalem. Some of the disciples are clinging to their old definition of Messiah. They expect thrones to be waiting for them in Jerusalem. None of them dream it will be crosses. The issue will come to a head at the Last Supper when Jesus will wordlessly address them by washing their feet (Jn 13).

For now, Jesus takes a child, perhaps one of Peter's children, and in a detail only provided by Mark, takes the child into his arms. Jesus radically identifies with powerless children. To welcome the child is to welcome him. To refuse the child is to refuse him. It is his way of engaging the disciples' imaginations, planting in their hearts the seed of a longing to identify themselves as children. It is an elegant argument against the desire for greatness.

SALTED WITH FIRE

38 John said to Him, "Teacher, we saw someone driving out demons in Your name, and we tried to stop him because he wasn't following us."

39 "Don't stop him," said Jesus, "because there is no one who will perform a miracle in My name who can soon afterward speak evil of Me. 40 For whoever is not against us is for us. 41 And whoever gives you a cup of water to drink because of My name, since you belong to the Messiah—I assure you: He will never lose his reward.

42 "But whoever causes the downfall of one of these little ones who believe in Me—it would be better for him if a heavy millstone were hung around his neck and he were thrown into the sea. 43 And if your hand causes your downfall, cut it off. It is better for you to enter life maimed than to have two hands and go to hell—the unquenchable fire, 44 [where

> *Their worm does not die,*
> *and the fire is not quenched.]*

45 And if your foot causes your downfall, cut it off. It is better for you to enter life lame than to have two feet and be thrown into hell—[the unquenchable fire, 46 where

Their worm does not die,
and the fire is not quenched.]

[47]And if your eye causes your downfall, gouge it out. It is better for you to enter the kingdom of God with one eye than to have two eyes and be thrown into hell, [48]where

Their worm does not die,
and the fire is not quenched.

[49]For everyone will be salted with fire. [50]Salt is good, but if the salt should lose its flavor, how can you make it salty? Have salt among yourselves and be at peace with one another."

*T*his is John's only speaking appearance in Mark's Gospel. We deduce that he was the youngest disciple because he lived so long that rumors about his great age circulated in the early church (see Jn 21:23). He lived into the reign of Trajan, which began in A.D. 98.[12] I imagine him as being so young that he is unaware of the others' humiliation. The disciples have seen someone successfully casting out demons in Jesus' name and forbidden him to continue. After all, this person was not one of the Twelve. This is ironic, since the disciples failed to cast the demon from the boy at the bottom of the mountain. Jesus tells them they should not have stopped the exorcist. It would be inconsistent for someone who does a miracle in Jesus' name to speak out against him later on. Jesus pronounces one of the maxims that become more frequent as they near Jerusalem: "Whoever is not against us is for us" (Mk 9:40).

It is an impressive achievement to cast out a demon. It is something the disciples have been unable to do. But, Jesus concludes, even those who offer a cup of water in his name will find their reward.

Then Jesus' mind returns to the exemplary child, who might still have been nestled contentedly in his arms. His expression darkens. He becomes mindful that his "little ones" will come under the attack of temptation. Whoever causes one of the little ones to stumble will be thrown into the sea with a large millstone tied around his neck. A few years earlier, the Romans did just that to a band of Galilean insurrectionists.

Jesus' emotions rise as he moves from that gruesome image to another that's still more gruesome. His language is hyperbolic, over the top. In the little time that remains, he wants to drive these final lessons home in a way the disciples will never forget.

They are unforgettable images: cutting off the hand or the foot, gouging out the eye. The painful alternative? Being thrown into hell. It would seem a reasonable thing to do to keep yourself from sin. No price is too great to pay to avoid that unimaginable place where "their worm does not die and the fire is not quenched."

This is an image from the final verse of the book of Isaiah. In some manuscripts, Jesus repeats the phrase three times (Mk 9:44, 46, 48). His tone is dark, filled with passion. He alternates his gaze between the child in his arms and the "little ones" who are his disciples. There is no language to express the colossal cost of sin. He will perfectly pay that price in a matter of weeks. It is a seed that must be planted in their hearts while there is still time.

With verse 49 the tone shifts. Could this be Mark's voice, or perhaps Peter's? It is a word addressed directly to Mark's Roman readers. Every one of them will be "salted with fire." Only Mark contains these words of caution. They are an echo of Peter's "fiery ordeal" (1 Pet 4:12). To be salted with fire is sacrificial language. Every follower of Jesus is to be a sacrifice for God. Though it might seem otherwise, this assault, this testing, is good. We cannot afford to lose it. The fire defines who we are in the world.

MARK 10

Four Questions

OF DIVORCE

10:1–16 The Pharisees try to trap Jesus.

OF SALVATION

10:17–31 A young man with an honest question.

OF SUFFERING

10:32–45 The cost of being a disciple.

OF FUNDAMENTAL NEED

10:46–52 The healing of Bartimaeus.

OF DIVORCE

¹He set out from there and went to the region of Judea and across the Jordan. Then crowds converged on Him again and, as He usually did, He began teaching them once more. ²Some Pharisees approached Him to test Him. They asked, "Is it lawful for a man to divorce [his] wife?"

³He replied to them, "What did Moses command you?"

⁴They said, "Moses permitted us to write divorce papers and send her away."

⁵But Jesus told them, "He wrote this commandment for you because of the hardness of your hearts. ⁶But from the beginning of creation God made them male and female.

> *⁷For this reason a man will leave*
> *his father and mother*
> *[and be joined to his wife],*
> *⁸and the two will become one flesh.*

So they are no longer two, but one flesh. ⁹Therefore what God has joined together, man must not separate."

¹⁰Now in the house the disciples questioned Him again about this matter. ¹¹And He said to them, "Whoever divorces his wife and marries another commits adultery against her. ¹²Also, if she divorces her husband and marries another, she commits adultery."

¹³Some people were bringing little children to Him so He might touch them, but His disciples rebuked them. ¹⁴When Jesus saw it, He was indignant and said to them, "Let the little children come to Me. Don't stop them, for the kingdom of God belongs to such as these. ¹⁵I assure you: Whoever does not welcome the kingdom of God like a little child will never enter it." ¹⁶After taking them in His arms, He laid His hands on them and blessed them.

What Luke requires ten chapters to tell, Mark gives us in one. Capernaum, home—all that is familiar—lies behind them. They cross over into Judea and it becomes clear that Jesus is on his way to Jerusalem. The ever-present crowds are there, less pressing and demanding, and as a result Jesus is able to teach unhindered. All along the Pharisees have been in the shadows, occasionally asking questions, pointing out violations of the law. Like a pack of hounds, they trail him everywhere. Now another question but not for the sake of information. It is a test.

The issue of divorce was a consistent topic of debate in the rabbinic community. The discussion hinged on a phrase in Deuteronomy 24:1: "If a man marries a woman, but she becomes displeasing to him because he finds something improper about her, he may write her a divorce certificate, hand it to her, and send her away from his house."

The central issue for the rabbis was the meaning of "something improper," or "shameful." There were two major schools of thought. The followers of Shammai, the stricter of the two schools, held that "shameful" referred only to adultery. Their conclusion? The only justifiable cause for divorce was marital unfaithfulness. The followers of Hillel, on the other hand, determined that "shameful" meant anything that annoyed or displeased the husband. It was a debate between polar opposites. Usually when there was a disagreement among the schools, often in regard to the Sabbath, Jesus sided with Hillel. This is the only example where he agrees with Shammai.

In rabbinic fashion, Jesus responds to their question first with his own question. To ask a Pharisee what Moses commanded on any topic was to receive a quick answer. The Pharisees respond by going straight to the point, referring to the primary passage of contention in Deuteronomy 24.

Jesus does not attack the Pharisees' position on divorce. Rather, his approach is to expand their definition of marriage. In the beginning God created them *ish* and *isha*, male and female—two separate entities that belong together, that were made to be one. The key concept in Jesus' understanding of marriage is oneness.

In the next three verses, as he provides his definition of marriage, Jesus uses four expressions to describe the idea of oneness: "be joined," "become one flesh," "no longer two, but one," and "what God has joined" (Mk 10:7-9). True marriage is the result of a God-created oneness that is impossible for man to disconnect or separate. How could a written certificate of divorce dissolve a bond that God has established? Mark gives no indication that the Pharisees disagreed with Jesus. Their test question has failed to produce the result they were looking for. We will hear no more from these Pharisees.

In Mark 10:10, Jesus and the disciples are in an unnamed house. We assume they have taken advantage of Jewish hospitality along the road to Jerusalem. The disciples, perhaps unsettled by Jesus' uncharacteristically severe position, ask him to explain. His statement is merely the logical conclusion of his initial premise. If true marriage is a God-created bond that man cannot break, then the conclusion is this: If someone divorces—that is, tries by human designs to break God's bond—and then remarries, that person has never truly divorced and so commits adultery. Jesus applies the principle to both men and women.

To those who have been abused by this verse, to those who have suffered through a divorce and then remarried, I believe the operative words in Mark 10:9 are "what God has joined together." Because of the hardness of the human heart, marriages occur that do not have as their foundation this bond created by God. Those marriages do not fall under Jesus' severe conclusion. But we must be cautious and preserve his original intent. If two people come together acknowledging that the Lord has bonded them and made them one, then when temptation arises to give up on that union, they must take seriously what Jesus said about the undissolvable bond God has created. The biblical provision for divorce is a sad concession God has made due to the hardness of our hearts, not his.

It is only natural that in close proximity to a discussion of the nature of marriage, Mark includes a pericope about children. For the second time in two chapters (see Mk 9:36), Jesus is physically holding children in his arms. Though the disciples rebuked the parents initially, thinking Jesus' time was too valuable to waste on children, Jesus (the emotional) is indignant. I like to believe that at this point in his life he might have needed to hold the children as much as they needed to be held by him.

OF SALVATION

17As He was setting out on a journey, a man ran up, knelt down before Him, and asked Him, "Good Teacher, what must I do to inherit eternal life?"

¹⁸"Why do you call Me good?" Jesus asked him. "No one is good but One—God. ¹⁹You know the commandments:

> *Do not murder;*
> *do not commit adultery;*
> *do not steal;*
> *do not bear false witness;*
> *do not defraud;*
> *honor your father and mother."*

²⁰He said to Him, "Teacher, I have kept all these from my youth."

²¹Then, looking at him, Jesus loved him and said to him, "You lack one thing: Go, sell all you have and give to the poor, and you will have treasure in heaven. Then come, follow Me." ²²But he was stunned at this demand, and he went away grieving, because he had many possessions.

²³Jesus looked around and said to His disciples, "How hard it is for those who have wealth to enter the kingdom of God!" ²⁴But the disciples were astonished at His words. Again Jesus said to them, "Children, how hard it is to enter the kingdom of God! ²⁵It is easier for a camel to go through the eye of a needle than for a rich person to enter the kingdom of God."

²⁶So they were even more astonished, saying to one another, "Then who can be saved?"

²⁷Looking at them, Jesus said, "With men it is impossible, but not with God, because all things are possible with God."

²⁸Peter began to tell Him, "Look, we have left everything and followed You."

²⁹"I assure you," Jesus said, "there is no one who has left house, brothers or sisters, mother or father, children, or fields because of Me and the gospel, ³⁰who will not receive 100 times more, now at this time—houses, brothers and sisters, mothers and children, and fields, with persecutions—and eternal life in the age to come. ³¹But many who are first will be last, and the last first."

The next question is neither a test nor a trap. It is a sincere request from a young man who genuinely wants to know. His sincerity is seen in his posture. He falls at Jesus' feet and addresses him respectfully as "good teacher." He asks a sincere question but still a flawed question. What must he do to inherit eternal life?

Jesus' first words are a challenge to the young man's concept of good. For him goodness is connected to performance—it is something he does. For Jesus, goodness belongs to God only. Notice that once more Jesus' first response to a question is another question. (It echoes his question to the Pharisees in Mark 10:3.) Responding to the young man at his own level, Jesus quotes the Commandments and receives precisely the response he has expected. "I have kept all these from my youth" (Mk 10:20).

Verse 21 is a precious window into the emotional life of Jesus. The word Mark uses for "looking" implies the act of seeing someone with your mind. I like to translate it "gazing." It is a form of the word the Gospels use to describe the distinctive way Jesus looks at Peter (Lk 22:61; Jn 1:42).

Jesus recognizes the man's sincerity. He is intimately acquainted with his world of works righteousness. Perhaps he is even touched by the man's sad delusion that the commandments are ultimately keepable. Two worlds meet in these two men. One sincerely seeks to inherit eternal life as a reward for his actions. The other has come to offer eternal life as a free and gracious gift.

Jesus' response, that the man should sell everything and follow him, is not the answer to the man's question. It is a litmus test that reveals the truth; he has not kept all the commandments. He has broken the first one and made money his god. His sad countenance and decision to walk away prove Jesus right. As Jesus watches the forlorn young man, he concludes something that is earth-shattering for the disciples: that it is difficult for the wealthy to enter the kingdom. "Children"—this is the first time he has called them that—"it is easier for a camel to go through the eye of a needle than for a rich person to enter the kingdom of God" (Mk 10:24-25).

A camel was the biggest animal in any of the disciples' imaginations. (I was once stuck on the back of a camel in Jerusalem. It felt like sitting on the roof of a house!) This is another hyperbolic image of impossibility. Try to imagine an elephant passing through a buttonhole. That, in Jesus' imagination, is easier than someone with great wealth entering the kingdom. A person does not enter the kingdom with anything—not with wealth, not with accomplishments, not with degrees. We come into the kingdom with one possession: the grace of Jesus Christ.

Still, if we are to engage with the passage and understand what lies behind the disciples' amazement, we need to step into their shoes. They come from the same world as the rich young man, where wealth is an unqualified blessing from God. Hence their disturbance at Jesus' words. In their world, poverty and sickness are punishments from God for sin. But Jesus has come to shatter this understanding of the Father. His embrace of and openness toward the poor and sick are his way of confronting the old system. As the rich man walks away dejected, Jesus has shattered yet another obsolete notion. If it is hard for rich men and women to enter the kingdom, the disciples moan, then "who can be saved?" (Mk 10:26). Jesus' reply? Saving is God's business. He makes all things possible.

The turning gears of Peter's mind are almost audible. He reminds Jesus of what he already knows: the disciples have left everything. And the truth is, they have. Jesus expands on this new value system. What they have left for his sake will be multiplied a hundred times in this present world. It is all upside down, Jesus says: "The first will be last, and the last first" (Mk 10:31).

Tradition says the rich young man eventually came back to Jesus. We may never know for sure, but one thing is certain: if he did come back, it was without his wealth.

OF SUFFERING

³²*They were on the road, going up to Jerusalem, and Jesus was walking ahead of them. They were astonished, but those who followed Him were afraid. Taking the Twelve aside again, He began to tell them the things that would happen to Him.*

³³*"Listen! We are going up to Jerusalem. The Son of Man will be handed over to the chief priests and the scribes, and they will condemn Him to death. Then they will hand Him over to the Gentiles, ³⁴and they will mock Him, spit on Him, flog Him, and kill Him, and He will rise after three days."*

³⁵*Then James and John, the sons of Zebedee, approached Him and said,*

"*Teacher, we want You to do something for us if we ask You.*"

36"What do you want Me to do for you?" He asked them.

37They answered Him, "Allow us to sit at Your right and at Your left in Your glory."

38But Jesus said to them, "You don't know what you're asking. Are you able to drink the cup I drink or to be baptized with the baptism I am baptized with?"

39"We are able," they told Him.

Jesus said to them, "You will drink the cup I drink, and you will be baptized with the baptism I am baptized with. 40But to sit at My right or left is not Mine to give; instead, it is for those it has been prepared for." 41When the [other] 10 [disciples] heard this, they began to be indignant with James and John.

42Jesus called them over and said to them, "You know that those who are regarded as rulers of the Gentiles dominate them, and their men of high positions exercise power over them. 43But it must not be like that among you. On the contrary, whoever wants to become great among you must be your servant, 44and whoever wants to be first among you must be a slave to all. 45For even the Son of Man did not come to be served, but to serve, and to give His life—a ransom for many."

Mark 10:32 is the first open indication that Jesus and the disciples are heading for Jerusalem. It is a poignant snapshot. Jesus is leading, which is probably the norm since he is a peripatetic rabbi. The disciples are "astonished." If we review all they have experienced in the last four or five chapters, this becomes clear. Their world is being turned upside down. Jesus has spoken repeatedly of his death and resurrection. Mark has made clear that they do not understand. Given their confusion, it is probable that they have no idea what waits for them in Jerusalem. Those who follow, we are told, are "afraid." It is a mixed crowd with mixed emotions making its way to the holy city. Along the way they would be joined by other Passover pilgrims and eventually blend into the river of souls making their way up to celebrate God's provision of the Passover lamb that was sacrificed for the sins of the people.

This is the third major statement by Jesus to the Twelve concerning his death. Of the three, it is the most detailed. It provides a virtual outline for Mark's Passion Week. Of the astonished disciples, two appear to be amazed at the prospect of going to Jerusalem and possibly taking part in Jesus' glory. It is a part of their stubborn definition of "Messiah." All Jesus' warnings have not been able to shift it. Their request: to sit at his right and left hand in his glory. In ancient culture, the seat at someone's right was reserved as the position of honor. The left-hand seat was for an intimate friend. In the least, this is a grotesquely inappropriate request. At most, it is a power play.

Jesus knows who will someday be at his right and left hand outside the walls of Jerusalem: two thieves hanging on crosses. "You don't know what you're asking," he says over his shoulder as he walks up the steep hill (Mk 10:38). In his value system, glory is a result of enduring suffering. Jesus asks if they can drink his cup and be baptized with his baptism. With thrones still blinding their eyes, they respond, "We are able" (Mk 10:39).

How supremely sad it must have been sometimes to know all that Jesus knew. These two brothers would be the first and the last to die for his sake. So he is forced to agree with them. But Jesus will claim no authority that does not belong to him. And so he pushes their question aside. The other ten disciples are understandably upset when they hear what James and John have asked. Jesus, knowing there is no time for dissension among them, understands that it is imperative that they pull together.

Mark 10:42-45 contains another statement of Jesus' radical new value system. He seeks to unite the disciples by appealing to their pride as Jewish men. He challenges them not to be like the Gentiles, who love to exercise authority over other people. Earlier he encouraged them to become like children; now he tells them they must become slaves. Why? Because he has come as a slave, has lived and will soon die like a slave; his death will provide the payment ("ransom") to purchase others who will become slaves as well (see Is 53).

OF FUNDAMENTAL NEED

46 They came to Jericho. And as He was leaving Jericho with His disciples and a large crowd, Bartimaeus (the son of Timaeus), a blind beggar, was sitting by the road. *⁴⁷When he heard that it was Jesus the Nazarene, he began to cry out, "Son of David, Jesus, have mercy on me!" ⁴⁸Many people told him to keep quiet, but he was crying out all the more, "Have mercy on me, Son of David!"*

⁴⁹Jesus stopped and said, "Call him."

So they called the blind man and said to him, "Have courage! Get up; He's calling for you." ⁵⁰He threw off his coat, jumped up, and came to Jesus.

⁵¹Then Jesus answered him, "What do you want Me to do for you?"

"Rabbouni," the blind man told Him, "I want to see!"

⁵²"Go your way," Jesus told him. "Your faith has healed you." Immediately he could see and began to follow Him on the road.

It will be the last overt miracle of the ministry of Jesus. It will lead to the last unlikely member of his followers. Compared to the rich young man, no one could be more dissimilar. He is poor. He is blind. Only Mark tells us his name: Bartimaeus.

We encounter him where we would expect to find a beggar—along the roadside. He sits in his own personal darkness, constantly bearing the condemnation of believing that his poverty and blindness are a curse, that they must have been a result of sin in his life. Jesus sees in him the perfect opportunity, a living parable of childlike helplessness. Unlike the rich young man, Bartimaeus knows there is nothing he can do to earn or deserve anything. At the moment he is asking neither for money nor forgiveness. When he hears that Jesus of Nazareth is passing by, he utters the perfect plea, the perfect prayer. Christians have been whispering it for centuries: "Have mercy."

They have rebuked the children; now the crowd tells the beggar to be quiet. But those who understand their need for mercy cannot be silenced so easily. Bartimaeus provides the perfect messianic moment. Jericho, only fifteen miles from Jerusalem, was called the "city of the palms." Here some of Jesus' followers will cut branches to wave and place at his feet when he enters the city. Jesus' time has come.

It follows Isaiah's script to perfection, beginning with the people telling the blind man to "take courage" (Mk 10:49; see Is 35:4-5). Mark gives us the detail that Bartimaeus throws aside his cloak—probably his only possession. With it he would have caught the coins for which he begged. Unlike the rich man, he spontaneously leaves everything he owns to come to Jesus.

Jesus asks Bartimaeus exactly the same question he asked James and John in verse 36: "What do you want Me to do for you?" (Mk 10:51). Do you sense the power of the moment? Remember all of the talk about having eyes and not seeing? It has all led up to this moment. It is perfect!

"I want to see," the blind man says (Mk 10:51).

In John's Gospel, Jesus says he has come into the world that those who do not see will see, and those who do see will become blind (Jn 9:39). Jesus heals Bartimaeus with the command "Go!" Not "Receive your sight," not even "Ephphatha," but simply "Go!" (Mk 10:52).

Bartimaeus becomes the jewel of Jesus' ministry. He is the one who was blind, who has asked for nothing else but mercy, who has left everything to "immediately" follow Jesus. He is the only person in Mark's Gospel who calls Jesus by his personal name (Mk 10:47)!

MARK 11

AN UNTRADITIONAL TRIUMPH

11:1–11 Jesus enters Jerusalem.

THE TEMPLE AND THE TREE

11:12–26 The expulsion from the temple.

A CONTEST OF QUESTIONS

11:27–33 Jesus' authority challenged.

AN UNTRADITIONAL TRIUMPH

¹When they approached Jerusalem, at Bethphage and Bethany near the Mount of Olives, He sent two of His disciples ²and told them, "Go into the village ahead of you. As soon as you enter it, you will find a young donkey tied there, on which no one has ever sat. Untie it and bring it here. ³If anyone says to you, 'Why are you doing this?' say, 'The Lord needs it and will send it back here right away.'"

⁴So they went and found a young donkey outside in the street, tied by a door. They untied it, ⁵and some of those standing there said to them, "What are you doing, untying the donkey?" ⁶They answered them just as Jesus had said, so they let them go. ⁷Then they brought the donkey to Jesus and threw their robes on it, and He sat on it.

⁸Many people spread their robes on the road, and others spread leafy branches cut from the fields. ⁹Then those who went ahead and those who followed kept shouting:

> *Hosanna!*
> *Blessed is He who comes*
> *in the name of the Lord!*
> *¹⁰Blessed is the coming kingdom*
> *of our father David!*
> *Hosanna in the highest heaven!*

¹¹And He went into Jerusalem and into the temple complex. After looking around at everything, since it was already late, He went out to Bethany with the Twelve.

The journey from Jericho to Jerusalem is an incredibly steep climb through the same desert region where Jesus endured temptation. We can scarcely imagine the feeling of relief the disciples must have experienced upon seeing the two small villages of Bethphage and Bethany. Mark is not precise about which village the disciples are sent to to borrow the donkey. Perhaps the village is Bethany and it is a donkey belonging to Martha, Mary and Lazarus (see Jn 11:1; 12:1). If anyone questions them about the donkey, the disciples are told to respond simply, "the Lord needs it" (Mk 11:3). This also implies that whoever owns the donkey is Jesus' acquaintance.

Note the detail in Mark 10:2 that no one had ever ridden the young donkey. This was a stipulation concerning ceremonial animals—they were not supposed to have ever labored (see Num 19:2; Deut 21:3; 1 Sam 6:7). The choice of a donkey's colt was symbolic of a king coming in peace. If, when a city was conquered, the victorious monarch approached riding a white warhorse, the inhabitants knew he was coming to judge and destroy the city. If he approached on a donkey's colt, they knew he was coming in peace (see Zech 9:9). A later rabbinic tradition said that when the Messiah returned, if Israel was not ready, he would ride a donkey's colt. If Israel was ready, he would ride a white horse.[13] The book of Revelation pictures Jesus' return on a white horse (Rev 6:2; 19:11)!

The reception Jesus receives as he enters Jerusalem clearly indicates that the crowd, perhaps only a small circle of his followers, believes he is coming as a king. The placing of their cloaks on the donkey and the spreading of the branches cut in the fields are reminiscent of the reception king Jehu received in 2 Kings 9:13.

The shouts, while they clearly demonstrate the mindset of his immediate followers, might also reflect the voices of others in the crowd who do not know who Jesus is. "Hosanna" and "Blessed is he who comes in the name of the Lord" (Mk 11:9 NIV) were common Passover greetings. During Passover the population of Jerusalem skyrocketed as righteous Jews who lived a prescribed distance from the city came to celebrate within the city walls. Jesus and his followers represent a relatively small clutch among this vast crowd.

More to the point, the so-called triumphal entry was less a triumph than we often imagine. According to Luke 19:41, Jesus was weeping as he entered the city. Amidst the confusion, shouts and mixed signals of kingship, Jesus is still wiping the tears from his eyes.

The detail in Mark 11:11, that Jesus entered the city, looked around and then returned to Bethany, is a detail only Peter remembered. It appears only in Mark's Gospel. The mention of Bethany is another hint that perhaps they were staying in the home of Lazarus.

Throughout the final week of the Passion narratives, it is important to keep in mind the setting. Jerusalem and its temple complex were not the weathered, beleaguered site we know today. The thirty-five-acre temple complex was the largest sacred enclosure in the Roman world, five times the area of the Acropolis in Athens. The top of the golden dome of the mosque that occupies the site today would have reached only the bottom of the doorsill of the Jewish temple. Some of its foundation stones were larger than any of the blocks of the pyramids in Egypt. The temple itself gleamed of white marble and pure gold. Had it been in existence earlier, it would have been on Herodotus's list of the seven wonders of the world.

THE TEMPLE AND THE TREE

[12] The next day when they came out from Bethany, He was hungry. [13] After seeing in the distance a fig tree with leaves, He went to find out if there was anything on it. When He came to it, He found nothing but leaves, because it was not the season for figs. [14] He said to it, "May no one ever eat fruit from you again!" And His disciples heard it.

[15] They came to Jerusalem, and He went into the temple complex and began to throw out those buying and selling in the temple. He overturned the money changers' tables and the chairs of those selling doves, [16] and would not permit anyone to carry goods through the temple complex.

[17] Then He began to teach them: "Is it not written, My house will be called a house of prayer for all nations? But you have made it a den of thieves!" [18] Then the chief priests and the scribes heard it and started looking for a way to destroy Him. For they were afraid of Him, because the whole crowd was astonished by His teaching.

[19] And whenever evening came, they would go out of the city.

[20] Early in the morning, as they were passing by, they saw the fig tree withered from the roots up. [21] Then Peter remembered and said to Him, "Rabbi, look! The fig tree that You cursed is withered."

[22] Jesus replied to them, "Have faith in God. [23] I assure you: If anyone says to this mountain, 'Be lifted up and thrown into the sea,' and does not doubt in his heart, but believes that what he says will happen, it will be done for him. [24] Therefore I tell you, all the things you pray and ask for—believe that

you have received them, and you will have them. ²⁵*And whenever you stand praying, if you have anything against anyone, forgive him, so that your Father in heaven will also forgive you your wrongdoing.* ²⁶*[But if you don't forgive, neither will your Father in heaven forgive your wrongdoing.]"*

*M*ark employs his bookend device for telling the story of the second temple expulsion. (The first is told only in John 2:12-25.) The bookends are composed of a two-part story of Jesus cursing the fig tree. It is a disturbing account when it is narrowly read out of context. People frequently observe that it is the only miracle of Jesus that involved the death of something (he did not directly cause the death of the two thousand pigs in Mark 5:13). It is also frequently pointed out how uncharacteristic, mean-spirited and unreasonable Jesus' actions were. A scan of the entire chapter and a sensitivity to the flow of the ministry reveals that the placement of the two parts of the story on either side of the account of the temple expulsion has a purpose. It indicates that one is intimately related to the other. Mark 11:12-21 is the story of the temple and the tree.

As the story opens in verse 12, we meet Jesus on his way in from Bethany. Mark tells us he is hungry. (Did Martha not prepare him a proper breakfast?) In the distance he sees a fig tree that has already leafed out. In this part of the world, fig trees sprout their leaves in March and April. They generally bear fruit in June. The Passion Week extends from the tenth to the seventeenth day of the Jewish month of Nisan (our late March and early April) in A.D. 33. Since the Jewish calendar is lunar and not solar like ours, the closest determination we can make is that this incident would have occurred sometime in March or April. It is early in the season, too early for figs, a fact that Mark makes note of. Out of his apparent frustration, Jesus says to the tree, "May no one ever eat fruit from you again" (Mk 11:14). Mark is careful to note that his disciples heard him say this. This is the first bookend: a hungry man, a green tree with no fruit, and his disappointment even though he knows it is not the season for figs.

Jesus makes his way down the Mount of Olives, crossing the Kidron

Valley, and enters through the double gate, ascending the shadowy staircase that opens out onto the vast temple complex. There, in the outermost court of the Gentiles, he finds a noisy marketplace. Mark mentions specifically the moneychangers and the sellers of doves as the objects of Jesus' anger.

In Jesus' day, moneychangers took in currencies from all over the area and exchanged them for the accepted currency of the temple, the shekel minted in Tyre. It was accepted for payment in the temple for two reasons: first, it was coined from the purest silver, and second, its value was the closest equivalent to the older Hebrew shekel. Past interpretations have tried to make the case that Jesus condemned the moneychangers because they were charging exorbitant exchange rates. In reality, the surcharge for the exchange was set by the temple authorities and was relatively small, covering only the devaluation due to the wearing away of the silver.[14] Jesus' anger probably had to do with the fact that the Tyrian coin bore the image of Herakles on one side and an inscription on the other that read, "Tyre, the holy and invincible."

The evidence as to why Jesus focused on the sellers of doves is clearer. Doves were the offering set aside for the poor (Lev 5:7). The Mishnah records that during Jesus' time, prices for doves in the temple market soared.[15] This accounts for Jesus' anger. Early in his ministry he proclaimed that he had come to preach good news to the poor (Lk 4:18).

Mark alone adds in verse 16 the detail that Jesus would not allow anyone to carry merchandise in the temple court. The Mishnah has this to say about respecting the temple area:

> A man should not behave himself unseemly while opposite the eastern gate [of the temple] since it faces toward the holy of holies. He may not enter into the Temple Mount with his staff or his sandal or his wallet, or with the dust upon his feet, nor may he make it a short by-path; still less may he spit there. (Berakoth 9:5)

The reference to the "short by-path" meant that no one should take a shortcut through the temple courts. Perhaps the merchants were coming and going, restocking their stalls with offerings and cutting through the courts.

Jesus' actions are clearly prophetic. Prophets such as Ezekiel, Isaiah and Jeremiah prophesied against abuses of the temple. Jesus quotes Isaiah, couching the quotation as a question: "Is it not written, My house will be called a house of prayer for all nations?" (Mk 11:17). "All nations" connects the quote to Jesus' location in the court of the Gentiles. This was as close as Gentile "God-fearers" could come to the temple. Yet the Jews had disrespectfully set up a marketplace there.

The first plot on Jesus' life began in Mark 3:6, after he healed a man in the synagogue of Capernaum on the Sabbath. Then it was a group of Pharisees together with some Herodians. Now it is the chief priests and scribes—more powerful and well-connected foes.[16] Mark closes the story by letting us know that Jesus leaves Jerusalem when evening comes. He does not specifically say he returns to Bethany. Perhaps after the confrontation with the chief priests, he begins sleeping in the garden of Gethsemane to avoid implicating his friends Mary, Martha and Lazarus.

The next morning, as they are traveling the same path back into the city, the disciples discover that the fig tree Jesus spoke to the day before has completely withered from the roots. Mark's witness, Peter, remembers what happened and points it out to Jesus, who turns the moment into a lesson on believing prayer. Jesus is standing on the Mount of Olives. "This mountain" is clearly what he is referring to in Mark 11:23. What seems to be a lesson on how to appropriate the power of prayer for personal needs turns out to be instruction on how to unleash the power of forgiveness.

The bookends that tell the story of the green and fruitless fig tree provide the context for understanding Jesus' prophetic actions in the temple. Jesus sees the world around him as a parable. When on the way to the temple he sees a green tree, even his human hunger becomes part of the parable. In Hosea 9:10 it is God who hungers for the early fruits of his people Israel. But the people become unfaithful and worship Baal. Knowing that a confrontation awaits him in the temple, Jesus speaks to the tree in a prophetic curse. What happens to the tree has already happened in the temple; the presence of the marketplace demonstrates it.

It is the prospect of going to the temple that day—that place so willfully, stubbornly fruitless, so full of religiosity, empty works and empty words—that lights the fuse of Jesus' smoldering frustration. For God, his Father, will always curse willful fruitlessness—theirs and ours.

A CONTEST OF QUESTIONS

[27] They came again to Jerusalem. As He was walking in the temple complex, the chief priests, the scribes, and the elders came [28] and asked Him, "By what authority are You doing these things? Who gave You this authority to do these things?"

[29] Jesus said to them, "I will ask you one question; then answer Me, and I will tell you by what authority I am doing these things. [30] Was John's baptism from heaven or from men? Answer Me."

[31] They began to argue among themselves: "If we say, 'From heaven,' He will say, 'Then why didn't you believe him?' [32] But if we say, 'From men'"—they were afraid of the crowd, because everyone thought that John was a genuine prophet. [33] So they answered Jesus, "We don't know."

And Jesus said to them, "Neither will I tell you by what authority I do these things."

*A*s Jesus and his disciples return to the "scene of the crime," they are confronted by the two groups that have been plotting to take his life, the chief priests and the scribes. The elders join them there. Though they have been referred to before in Mark (Mk 7:3; 8:31) this is the first time we actually meet them. These three groups make up the Sanhedrin, or Jewish ruling council. The Twelve and also Paul will come into conflict with the Sanhedrin in the book of Acts (Acts 5:21; 6:12; 22:30).

There must be some indication of tension at Jesus' return. Perhaps one of the merchants from the day before, recognizing Jesus, has begun to pack up his goods. Notice that no one openly condemns what he did. The Jewish leaders' only question is one of authority: "Who gave You this authority to do these things?" (Mk 11:28).

Of all the Pharisaic groups and scribes with which Jesus has locked horns, this is the most powerful and adroit. He responds in rabbinic form with a question. This will be a contest of questions. If they can answer his question, he will answer theirs. It is an offer they cannot refuse.

Jesus asks his own question about authority concerning his cousin John the Baptist: "Was John's baptism from heaven or from man?" (Mk 11:30). It is a brilliant question. The leaders see it as a trap, like one of their questions. Either answer will land them in trouble. It is unanswerable. Whether Jesus intended it as a trap or not, their answer about John's authority to baptize will determine their conclusion regarding Jesus' authority. They respond with three words they are loath to say: "We don't know" (Mk 11:33). Their inability to answer frees Jesus from having to respond to their question.

Think of this first encounter with the members of the Sanhedrin as a "dry run." In Mark 12, along with the Pharisees and Sadducees, they will lay more traps for Jesus. They will reappear in the garden when he is arrested in Mark 14:43. Together, they will lead him to Pilate in Mark 15:1.

MARK 12

Final Questions

WHAT WILL HE DO?

12:1-12 The parable of the tenants.

TO CAESAR OR NOT?

12:13-17 The question of paying taxes.

WHOSE WILL SHE BE?

12:18-27 The question of marriage and resurrection.

THE GREATEST COMMANDMENT?

12:28-34 An honest question.

WHOSE SON IS THE CHRIST?

12:35-40 Jesus silences his accusers.

THE WIDOW'S OFFERING

12:41-44 Jesus redefines generosity.

WHAT WILL HE DO?

[1] Then He began to speak to them in parables: "A man planted a vineyard, put a fence around it, dug out a pit for a winepress, and built a watchtower. Then he leased it to tenant farmers and went away. [2] At harvest time he sent a slave to the farmers to collect some of the fruit of the vineyard from the farmers. [3] But they took him, beat him, and sent him away empty-handed. [4] Again he sent another slave to them, and they hit him on the head and treated him shamefully. [5] Then he sent another, and they killed that one. [He] also [sent] many others; they beat some and they killed some.

[6] "He still had one to send, a beloved son. Finally he sent him to them, saying, 'They will respect my son.'

[7] "But those tenant farmers said among themselves, 'This is the heir. Come, let's kill him, and the inheritance will be ours!' [8] So they seized him, killed him, and threw him out of the vineyard.

[9] "Therefore, what will the owner of the vineyard do? He will come and destroy the farmers and give the vineyard to others. [10] Haven't you read this Scripture:

> *The stone that the builders rejected—*
> *this has become the cornerstone.*
> *[11] This came from the Lord*
> *and is wonderful in our eyes?"*

[12] Because they knew He had said this parable against them, they were looking for a way to arrest Him, but they were afraid of the crowd. So they left Him and went away.

The contest of questions in the previous chapter (Mk 11:27-33) was merely the prelude to what would become a series of five questions in chapter 12. Jesus silenced all three groups allied against him with an unanswerable question concerning John's baptism. Now he will tell a prophetic parable that concludes with another question—a question Jesus himself will uncharacteristically answer.

This parable is usually referred to as the "parable of the tenants" and is based on a beautiful song in Isaiah 5:1-7. In the song, the prophet sings to the one he loves: God. In his vision, the Lord has planted a vineyard on a fertile hillside. He hopes for a crop of good grapes, but it yields only bad ones. The dark song goes on to speak of judgment, of the protective wall around the vineyard being torn down, of rain being withheld, of destruction.

In Jesus' parable, it is simply a "man" who goes through the laborious preparations involved in planting a vineyard. He rents it to some farmers and leaves on a journey. In Jesus' day, absentee landlords were common, especially in the fertile area of Galilee, and landlords were paid rent based on a portion of the harvest. The images in this story were readily available in Jesus' listeners' experience. When the landlord in the parable sends one of his servants to collect what is due him, the servant is beaten and sent away. One after another the landlord sends his servants to collect what he is owed. Each one is beaten; some are murdered. Throughout Scripture, the term "servant" is a code word for prophet (see Jer 7:25; Ezek 38:17; Dan 6:9; Amos 3:7; Zech 1:6). Jesus' parable reaches back into Israel's history even as it looks forward into what will become his own experience in a matter of days.

Out of desperation, the naïve landlord decides to send his beloved son, thinking the tenants will recognize his authority and respect him. But the tenants conclude that if the son is coming, the father must have died. If he is out of the picture, they can claim the vineyard for themselves. So they murder the son, throwing his body out of the vineyard. The final insult, neglecting even to bury him, would have represented a particular outrage in Jewish culture. It is an engaging story, designed to disgust the listeners. In Luke's version, someone in the crowd blurts out, "No—never!" (Lk 20:16).

Now comes the first of five questions in this chapter. It is Jesus' question, "What will the owner of the vineyard do?" (Mk 12:9). Rarely does Jesus answer his own question, but here his response provides the perfect climax to the outrage of the parable. The owner will kill the tenants, says Jesus, and give the vineyard to others. The majority of the listeners may or may not recognize the source of the story as Isaiah's song, but there is no question that the priests and scribes understand. They are about to be kicked out of their own party.

I imagine Jesus' final words being spoken in the simmering silence of the crowd. The common folk are outraged by the story, the religious leaders infuriated by its deeper implications. Then Jesus uses another code word, one that refers back to Psalm 118:22-23. Earlier the word "servant" had a dual meaning. This word, "stone" (*eben*), sounds much like the word for "son" (*ben*). The rejected stone is code for the rejected son. The presence of this statement in Mark is another of Peter's fingerprints on the text. His understanding of Jesus as the stone was fundamental to the way he perceived Jesus, himself and the community of believers.

> Coming to him, a living stone—rejected by men but chosen and valuable to God—you yourselves, as living stones, are being built into a spiritual house for a holy priesthood to offer spiritual sacrifices acceptable to God through Jesus Christ. For it stands in Scripture:

> Look! I lay a stone in Zion,
> a chosen and valuable cornerstone,
> and the one who believes in Him
> will never be put to shame!

> So the honor is for you who believe; but for the unbelieving,

> The stone that the builders rejected—
> this One has become the cornerstone,

> and

> A stone that causes men to stumble,
> and a rock that trips them up. (1 Pet 2:4-8)

We learned in Mark 11:18 that the grim alliance of scribes, priests and Pharisees had decided to kill Jesus. Now, for the first time, we are told that their plan begins with an arrest.

TO CAESAR OR NOT?

13 Then they sent some of the Pharisees and the Herodians to Him to trap Him by what He said. 14 When they came, they said to Him, "Teacher, we know You are truthful and defer to no one, for You don't show partiality but teach truthfully the way of God. Is it lawful to pay taxes to Caesar or not? 15 Should we pay, or should we not pay?"

But knowing their hypocrisy, He said to them, "Why are you testing Me? Bring Me a denarius to look at." ¹⁶So they brought one. "Whose image and inscription is this?" He asked them.

"Caesar's," they said.

¹⁷Then Jesus told them, "Give back to Caesar the things that are Caesar's, and to God the things that are God's." And they were amazed at Him.

*N*ow that the plot against Jesus has been set in motion, the word "they" in Mark's Gospel begins to refer to the three-part league that has come together against him: the chief priests, the scribes and the elders. "They" will trail Jesus like a dark shadow. "They" will try to trap him with questions, hoping for something—anything—on which to base a charge against him.

It only makes sense that they would begin the assault with their best shot. If they can trick Jesus into implicating himself by any negative statement against the Romans, it will be easy enough to formulate a charge against him. The question of paying taxes to Caesar was a particularly sensitive one. In Acts 5:37, we learn that another Galilean, Judas, was killed by the Romans for inciting a rebellion. For now, their deepest hope is that Jesus' answer will cause him to follow Judas to the cross.

When we consider the dual aspect of the trap, it becomes clear why the conspirators have sent both Pharisees and Herodians. These two groups represent the polar extremes of the possible answers to the question. If Jesus sides with the Pharisees and says that taxes should not be paid to Rome, the Herodians will be there as witnesses against him. (The Jews have been paying tribute to Rome since Jesus was a small boy in A.D. 6.) If Jesus sides with the Herodians and supports the payment of taxes, the Pharisees are there to testify against him. It is the perfect question with which to trap him. They are the perfect witnesses.

Jesus asks to be shown a coin. Remember that zealous Jews would neither look at nor even touch a Roman coin. His dual question provides the key to understanding this exchange. Jesus asks whose "image" and whose "inscription" is on the coin (Mk 12:16). The image would have portrayed Tiberius, who became emperor when Jesus was about fourteen years old. The inscription would have claimed him to be a god: "Tiberius Caesar, the Divine Augustus."

When Jesus' questioners respond to his question about the image and inscription with "Caesar's," it is Jesus who springs a trap. The Pharisees and Herodians are caught when Jesus blithely states, "Give back to Caesar the things that are Caesar's, and to God the things that are God's" (Mk 12:17).

This statement of Jesus' is often used to justify a Christian's responsibility to pay taxes. While other verses in the New Testament clearly posit our responsibility to be subject to civil authority (Rom 13:1-6; 1 Pet 2:13), this verse is probably not one of them. Given Jesus' reference to the inscription, his statement would imply that nothing belongs to Caesar and everything to God.

It is an elegant answer. It leaves no opportunity for the Herodians to concoct a charge of inciting a tax rebellion, nor can the Pharisees create a blasphemy charge from Jesus' brilliant response. This initial attack is a failure. Another trap will be laid by yet another group determined to see Jesus dead.

WHOSE WILL SHE BE?

18 Some Sadducees, who say there is no resurrection, came to Him and questioned Him: 19 "Teacher, Moses wrote for us that if a man's brother dies, leaves his wife behind, and leaves no child, his brother should take the wife and produce offspring for his brother. 20 There were seven brothers. The first took a wife, and dying, left no offspring. 21 The second also took her, and he died, leaving no offspring. And the third likewise. 22 The seven also left no offspring. Last of all, the woman died too. 23 In the resurrection, when they rise, whose wife will she be, since the seven had married her?"

24 Jesus told them, "Are you not deceived because you don't know the Scriptures or the power of God? 25 For when they rise from the dead, they neither marry nor are given in marriage but are like angels in heaven. 26 Now concerning the dead being raised—haven't you read in the book of Moses, in the passage about the burning bush, how God spoke to him: I am the God of Abraham and the God of Isaac and the God of Jacob? 27 He is not God of the dead but of the living. You are badly deceived."

*T*his is the only reference to the Sadducees in Mark's Gospel. Matthew refers to them seven times, Luke once and John not at all. At this moment in Jewish history they were a powerful sect, exercising control of the priesthood. Their name is derived from one of the high priests, Zadok, whose name is based on the Hebrew word for "just" (*saddiq*). Their power over the priestly caste in Jerusalem led the people to refer to priests not as sons of Aaron but sons of Zadok.[17] They considered the five books of Moses to be the only authoritative Scripture, rejecting the Prophets and the Writings. They found no reference to angels or the resurrection in the Torah and therefore rejected both, hence Mark's parenthetical statement in verse 18. Their hypocrisy is clear: their trap question is based on the resurrection, in which they do not believe.

The reference to what "Moses wrote" (Mk 12:19) concerns Levirate marriage, a legal provision in the Torah that allowed a brother to marry the wife of his deceased brother and have children by her (Deut 25:5-10). This would ensure that the deceased's name would not die out in Israel. It is a straightforward provision to protect the bloodline in a nation whose survival depended on the continuation of family descent.

In the Sadducees' story, the first of the seven brothers marries but dies childless. In succession the remaining brothers marry the woman and also die without children. Finally, the wife passes away. At the resurrection, when they are trying to sort out this complicated relationship, whose wife will this woman be? (The Pharisees concluded elsewhere that she would remain the first brother's wife.)

Jesus' response is a cold slap in the faces of the Sadducees. To say these men do not know the Scriptures is a serious insult. Neither, says Jesus, do they know the power of God. The two are inseparable. Jesus does not directly answer the question. Instead he dismantles the assumption upon which it is based. Resurrection is not simply reanimation. It represents complete transformation, including the transformation of human relationships. Resurrected men and women will live, like the angels, in a relational framework that supersedes marriage.

In Mark 12:26, Jesus attacks the Sadducees' disbelief in resurrection, and his assault is all the more devastating because he uses a passage from their own Scriptures (Ex 3:6). His words "Haven't you read in the book of Moses" would have taken their breath away. Indeed, Mark records that they are silent from this moment on.

The logical steps of Jesus' very rabbinic argument are not immediately discernible to many of us. In his first premise, Jesus establishes the fact that God spoke of himself to Moses as the God of Abraham, Isaac and Jacob. We need to remember that the three patriarchs were already dead. Next, Jesus posits that God is not the God of the dead but of the living, quickly concluding, "You are badly deceived" (Mk 12:27). You and I might be a bit confused about how this argument wordlessly concludes with a validation of bodily resurrection. The missing step is simple. If God speaks of the deceased patriarchs in the present tense, and if he is the God of the living, then those patriarchs and indeed everyone who has ever died is alive to him in the present moment and will arise when he returns. After all, God does not tie his name to corpses.

THE GREATEST COMMANDMENT?

28 One of the scribes approached. When he heard them debating and saw that Jesus answered them well, he asked Him, "Which commandment is the most important of all?"

29 "This is the most important," Jesus answered:

Listen, Israel! The Lord our God, the Lord is One. 30 Love the Lord your God with all your heart, with all your soul, with all your mind, and with all your strength.

31 "The second is: Love your neighbor as yourself. There is no other commandment greater than these."

32 Then the scribe said to Him, "You are right, Teacher! You have correctly said that He is One, and there is no one else except Him. 33 And to love Him with all your heart, with all your understanding, and with all your strength, and to love your neighbor as yourself, is far more important than all the burnt offerings and sacrifices."

34 When Jesus saw that he answered intelligently, He said to him, "You are not far from the kingdom of God." And no one dared to question Him any longer.

*T*he final trap question comes at Jesus from another direction. First it was the Pharisees and Herodians in Mark 12:13-17, then the Sadducees in verses 18-27. Now it is one of the scribes. While Pharisees, Sadducees and Herodians were political parties or sects, "scribes" (*grammateus*) represented a profession. A scribe could be a member of the Pharisees or Sadducees. They were specialists at interpreting the Scriptures, ordained sometime after their fortieth birthday. Scribes were accorded the right to sit with the Sanhedrin. They were also sometimes referred to as lawyers (*nomikos*).

In Matthew 22:34-35, this particular scribe is a member of the Pharisees. Matthew also makes it clear that this final question is also a trap. Mark presents the story as a more neutral encounter, stating that the scribe has recognized the wisdom of Jesus' answer. The scribe's question is a popular one. In the first century, Judaism acknowledged 613 separate commandments. It was said that the prophet Amos reduced all the commandments to one. In essence, the scribe is asking Jesus to do the same thing.

Jesus responds first with the central creed of Judaism, known as the "Shema" (Deut 6:4-5). It is the foundational doctrine of monotheism: "Listen, Israel: the LORD our God, the LORD is One." After the statement comes the command to love the God who is one with all that we are—all our heart, soul, mind and strength. If there is an acceptable answer to the question, surely the Shema is it.

In the second part of his answer, Jesus quotes Leviticus 19:18: "Love your neighbor as yourself." In Luke 10 another scribe asked Jesus what he must do to inherit eternal life and received the same two verses from Deuteronomy and Leviticus as an answer. In Jesus' mind the two are one, inseparable. One cannot love the God who is one without, as an expression of that love, loving one's neighbor (see 1 Jn 4:20). The scribe appreciates and approves of Jesus' answer. He expertly inserts a passing reference to 1 Samuel:

> Does the LORD takes pleasure in burnt offerings and sacrifices
> as much as in obeying the LORD?
> Look: to obey is better than sacrifice,
> to pay attention [is better] than the fat of rams. (1 Sam 15:22)

Whether the scribe is sincere or not, he receives a sincere response from Jesus. According to Jesus, he is close to the kingdom. He has begun to understand the foundations of loving God and neighbor.

WHOSE SON IS THE CHRIST?

[35] So Jesus asked this question as He taught in the temple complex, "How can the scribes say that the Messiah is the Son of David? [36] David himself says by the Holy Spirit:

> *The Lord declared to my Lord,*
> *'Sit at My right hand*
> *until I put Your enemies under Your feet.'*

[37] David himself calls Him 'Lord'; how then can the Messiah be his Son?" And the large crowd was listening to Him with delight.

[38] He also said in His teaching, "Beware of the scribes, who want to go around in long robes, and who want greetings in the marketplaces, [39] the front seats in the synagogues, and the places of honor at banquets. [40] They devour widows' houses and say long prayers just for show. These will receive harsher punishment."

*T*he previous pericope ended with the statement, "And no one dared to question Him any longer" (Mk 12:34). In case anyone is waiting in the wings with another verbal trap, Jesus poses one last unanswerable question. (Matthew 22:46 confirms that the dilemma posed by Jesus ended their questions for good!) The fifth and final question in Mark 12 belongs to Jesus.

He begins by quoting the scholars, the "religious professionals." They rightly call the Messiah the "son of David." It is Matthew's favorite designation for the Messiah. In Mark's Gospel the name only occurs twice, here and in Mark 10:47-48 as the blind man calls out to Jesus. (The term "son of David" is not found in the Old Testament as a designation for the Messiah, although the Davidic connection to the Messiah is clear in the prophets [see Is 9:7; 11:1; Jer 23:5; Hos 3:5].)

In one of the psalms, David wrote:

The LORD declared to my Lord:
"Sit at my right hand." (Ps 110:1)

The first "Lord" is a reference to God himself. The second refers to the
Messiah, whose enemies will be placed underneath his feet, a reference
to his great victory. David, the writer of the psalm, refers to the messianic son of David as his Lord. It is a conundrum. Jesus is exposing the
fact that even the experts don't really understand who the Messiah is.
The scribes must have been offended by this as well. Mark tells us the
crowd was delighted!

Having exposed their lack of basic biblical understanding, Jesus proceeds to warn the crowd against those who pose as experts in the law.
They are easily recognizable by their white flowing robes. They revel in
the perks of their exalted position in Jewish society. But, says Jesus,
they sponge off helpless widows.

As a postscript to Mark 12:40, Mark will give us a snapshot of just
such a widow and how her poverty produced the perfect gift.

THE WIDOW'S OFFERING

*⁴¹Sitting across from the temple treasury, He watched how the crowd
dropped money into the treasury. Many rich people were putting in large
sums. ⁴²And a poor widow came and dropped in two tiny coins worth very
little. ⁴³Summoning His disciples, He said to them, "I assure you: This poor
widow has put in more than all those giving to the temple treasury. ⁴⁴For
they all gave out of their surplus, but she out of her poverty has put in everything she possessed—all she had to live on."*

I love imagining Jesus sitting and "people-watching" near the offering
chests in the court of the women. The Mishnah speaks of "shofar-
chests"—that is, offering boxes with trumpet-shaped openings. As he
watches with the silent disciples, they observe the rich patrons of the
temple throwing in their large, clanging offerings.

To be able to engage with the text we must realize just how minuscule the widow's coins were. Mark identifies them as *lepta*, from the Greek word *leptos* for "thin." These were the smallest denominations minted, containing 1.55 grams of copper. If you were to place one in the open palm of your hand, you could blow it away like a feather. That the widow places "two" coins is significant. She could have kept one for herself. She does not.

I also love the fact that Jesus points her out as an exemplar to his disciples. In terms of his upside-down value system, where the first are last and the last first, she has just placed a vast fortune in the shofar chest. The last and the least shall be the first and the richest in the kingdom. Jesus happily points to her as one whose poverty has produced the greatest of gifts.

There is a story in the rabbinic literature in a commentary on Leviticus that is reminiscent of Mark's story of the widow. It reveals that Jesus' radical value system was reflected in some of the rabbis' teaching: "A priest rejected the offering of a handful of grain from a poor widow. That night in the dream he was commanded: 'Do not despise her. It is as if she had offered her life.'"[18]

MARK 13

The Simplicity of Jesus' End-Time Teaching

THE FATE OF THE MASSIVE STONES!

¹As He was going out of the temple complex, one of His disciples said to Him, "Teacher, look! What massive stones! What impressive buildings!"

²Jesus said to him, "Do you see these great buildings? Not one stone will be left here on another that will not be thrown down!"

³While He was sitting on the Mount of Olives across from the temple complex, Peter, James, John, and Andrew asked Him privately, ⁴"Tell us, when will these things happen? And what will be the sign when all these things are about to take place?"

⁵Then Jesus began by telling them: "Watch out that no one deceives you. ⁶Many will come in My name, saying, 'I am He,' and they will deceive many. ⁷When you hear of wars and rumors of wars, don't be alarmed; these things must take place, but the end is not yet. ⁸For nation will rise up against nation, and kingdom against kingdom. There will be earthquakes in various places, and famines. These are the beginning of birth pains.

⁹"But you, be on your guard! They will hand you over to sanhedrins, and you will be flogged in the synagogues. You will stand before governors and kings because of Me, as a witness to them. ¹⁰And the good news must first be proclaimed to all nations. ¹¹So when they arrest you and hand you over, don't worry beforehand what you will say. On the contrary, whatever is given to you in that hour—say it. For it isn't you speaking, but the Holy Spirit. ¹²Then brother will betray brother to death, and a father his child. Children will rise up against parents and put them to death. ¹³And you will be hated by everyone because of My name. But the one who endures to the end will be delivered.

¹⁴"When you see the abomination that causes desolation standing where it should not" (let the reader understand), "then those in Judea must flee to the mountains! ¹⁵A man on the housetop must not come down or go in to get anything out of his house. ¹⁶And a man in the field must not go back to get his clothes. ¹⁷Woe to pregnant women and nursing mothers in those days! ¹⁸Pray it won't happen in winter. ¹⁹For those will be days of tribulation, the kind that hasn't been from the beginning of the world, which God created, until now and never will be again! ²⁰Unless the Lord limited those days, no one would survive. But He limited those days because of the elect, whom He chose.

²¹"Then if anyone tells you, 'Look, here is the Messiah! Look—there!' do not believe it! ²²For false messiahs and false prophets will rise up and will perform signs and wonders to lead astray, if possible, the elect. ²³And you must watch! I have told you everything in advance."

*W*ith the image of the poor widow and her extravagant gift still fresh in his experience, Jesus makes his way out of the temple complex to the relative simplicity and quiet of the Mount of Olives. As they make their way, the disciples point out the massive stones, some weighing one hundred tons and more. (The heaviest stones in the pyramids are a mere two and a half tons.) The disciples direct Jesus' attention to the magnificence of the marble- and gold-clad buildings (see appendix C). In their Galilean backwater simplicity, the disciples are in awe of the enormous thirty-five-acre complex. But they have seen these wonders on more than one occasion. It makes me wonder if they are just making small talk in an attempt to distract Jesus. Jesus will not be distracted. Looking up at the massive façade of the temple, he whispers the double negative: "No, not one stone will be left here on another" (Mk 13:2, author's translation). To the Twelve it sounds like the end of the world.

They cross the valley and make their way to one of the groves on the Mount of Olives overlooking the gleaming temple complex. Sitting at his feet are the first four disciples, Peter, James, John and Andrew. They are still trying to recover from the shock of Jesus' prophecy. If we are to understand Jesus' answers, we must listen closely to the disciples' two questions. The first: "When will these things happen?" The second: "What will be the sign when all these things are about to take place?" (Mk 13:4). To these two questions Jesus will provide two clearly separate answers.

The first question involves the fulfillment of Jesus' shocking prediction regarding the stones of the temple, that not one stone would be upon another. Jesus provides four signposts that point to the destruction of the temple in A.D. 70.

- There will be false messiahs, but the disciples should not allow themselves to be deceived (Mk 13:5, 21-23).

- There will be wars and rumors of wars, but the disciples need to understand that such things happen (Mk 13:7).

- There will be earthquakes and famines, but these are only the beginning (Mk 13:8).

- The disciples will be persecuted, but the gospel must first be preached to all nations (Mk 13:9-11).

In verse 12, Mark records a prophecy that would have resonated in the ears of his Roman readers as they suffered under Nero's persecution. Families would split as brothers betrayed brothers, fathers betrayed children and children betrayed parents. What's more, the disciples would be hated by everyone because of their commitment to Jesus.

Each detail of Jesus' words found its fulfillment in the four decades leading up to the destruction of the temple in A.D. 70. Five major earthquakes occurred: in Crete (A.D. 46), Rome (A.D. 51), Phrygia (A.D. 53, 60) and Camponia (A.D. 63). There were three great famines during the reign of Claudius: in Judea (A.D. 44), Greece (A.D. 50) and Rome (A.D. 52). In addition, A.D. 65 was the worst year for famines and earthquakes in the entire history of Rome, and A.D. 69, known as the "year of the four emperors," was a time of political confusion and upheaval the likes of which Rome had never experienced. The book of Acts records the arrests and trials of Jesus' apostles. Jesus has provided an accurate description of their experience from the present time until the years just prior to A.D. 70. Such things must happen, Jesus says, "but the end is not yet" (Mk 13:7).

In Mark 13:14, Jesus' tone shifts. He moves from generalities to specifics, describing the events directly surrounding Titus's destruction of the temple in A.D. 70. The "abomination that causes desolation" can refer to any number of events. The phrase comes from Daniel 9:27 and was first fulfilled in December of 167 B.C. when Antiochus IV placed a statue of Zeus on the altar of burnt offerings in the court of the temple. Jesus' prophecy most likely refers to the moment when Titus and his soldiers set up altars in the temple area and offered sacrifices to pagan gods after the defeat of the Jewish rebels. Some believe the abomination came when, in A.D. 68, the Zealots anointed a clown as high priest. The Jewish Christians recognized this as the sign Jesus had spoken of and fled to the city of Pella before Jerusalem was cut off by the Roman tenth legion.[19]

With the parenthetical statement "let the reader understand," Jesus begins to describe the distinguishing characteristic of the prophetic answer to the disciples' first question; "these things" will be something you can run away from. They must flee to the mountains, not even taking the time to gather up their possessions (Mk 13:15-16). The flight will be particularly difficult for young women and mothers who are pregnant. It will be the worst calamity they have ever experienced. But, Jesus continues in Mark 13:21-23, as much as the destruction of the temple will seem like the end of the world, the Messiah will not return at that point. He concludes his first answer clearly in verse 23 with the command to "Watch!"

A DRAMATIC SHIFT

[24] "But in those days, after that tribulation:

> *The sun will be darkened,*
> *and the moon will not shed its light;*
> *[25] the stars will be falling from the sky,*
> *and the celestial powers will be shaken.*

[26] Then they will see the Son of Man coming in clouds with great power and glory. [27] He will send out the angels and gather His elect from the four winds, from the end of the earth to the end of the sky.

[28] "Learn this parable from the fig tree: As soon as its branch becomes tender and sprouts leaves, you know that summer is near. [29] In the same way, when you see these things happening, know that He is near—at the door! [30] I assure you: This generation will certainly not pass away until all these things take place. [31] Heaven and earth will pass away, but My words will never pass away."

*I*n verse 24 Jesus' language shifts dramatically. Before, he was describing an earthly event, something his disciples could run away from. Now he answers their second question, "What will be the sign when all these things are about to take place?" His language becomes apocalyptic. He begins to speak in prophetic poetry about the sun, moon, clouds and winds. He warned them earlier not to be deceived when others would say the Messiah had come, but now he gives them a vivid description. He will come in the clouds with the angels, gathering the elect. The vocabulary of his two answers could not be more different. Two questions were asked, and two answers were given: one cataclysmic but earthly, the other universal.

In an instant Jesus brings the disciples back to the present moment, from celestial catastrophe to the familiar shady grove that overlooks the temple still lying untouched across the valley. He is holding the branch of a leafy fig tree. It is a parable, says Jesus, for whom all of life is a living parable. When the leaves are green, summer has come. Likewise, when you see the signposts he has spoken of happening all around, know that the time has come. It is that simple. Though heaven and earth will dissolve as he has just described, his words will never pass away.

MORE THAN KNOWING

32 "Now concerning that day or hour no one knows—neither the angels in heaven nor the Son—except the Father. 33 Watch! Be alert! For you don't know when the time is [coming]. 34 It is like a man on a journey, who left his house, gave authority to his slaves, gave each one his work, and commanded the doorkeeper to be alert. 35 Therefore be alert, since you don't know when the master of the house is coming—whether in the evening or at midnight or at the crowing of the rooster or early in the morning. 36 Otherwise, he might come suddenly and find you sleeping. 37 And what I say to you, I say to everyone: Be alert!"

The disciples have asked their questions and received their answers. But for Jesus, much more is involved in following him than simply knowing the answers. Beyond all knowing lies the faith that manifests itself through obedience. His final words on the subject aren't about specific signs but rather obedience. Three times in five verses (Mk 13:33-37) he mentions staying awake or alert. Inexplicably, he confesses that even the Son does not know the day or the hour. Could it be that in his characteristic, humble servanthood the Son has chosen not to know? Is Jesus' own confession proof that there is more than knowing? Is his life not a parable of obedient service?

Again the image of the slave surfaces in Jesus' language. The disciples, Jesus says in this brief, three-verse parable, should be like slaves who have been given two things from their master: authority and work to do. Knowing when the master might return is not their concern, only faithful service. Knowing is not what matters. Obedience is everything.

MARK 14

THE ANOINTING

14:1-11 Jesus anointed at Bethany.

THE LORD'S SUPPER

14:12-26 Jesus and the disciples share Passover.

THE EMOTIONAL UNRAVELING OF PETER

14:27-31 Jesus predicts denial.

ABBA

14:32-42 Jesus prays in the garden.

THE KISS

14:43-52 Judas's betrayal.

I AM

14:53-72 Jesus before the Sanhedrin.

THE ANOINTING

¹After two days it was the Passover and the Festival of Unleavened Bread. The chief priests and the scribes were looking for a treacherous way to arrest and kill Him. ²"Not during the festival," they said, "or there may be rioting among the people."

³While He was in Bethany at the house of Simon who had a serious skin disease, as He was reclining at the table, a woman came with an alabaster jar of pure and expensive fragrant oil of nard. She broke the jar and poured it on His head. ⁴But some were expressing indignation to one another: "Why has this fragrant oil been wasted? ⁵For this oil might have been sold for more than 300 denarii and given to the poor." And they began to scold her.

⁶Then Jesus said, "Leave her alone. Why are you bothering her? She has done a noble thing for Me. ⁷You always have the poor with you, and you can do what is good for them whenever you want, but you do not always have Me. ⁸She has done what she could; she has anointed My body in advance for burial. ⁹I assure you: Wherever the gospel is proclaimed in the whole world, what this woman has done will also be told in memory of her."

¹⁰Then Judas Iscariot, one of the Twelve, went to the chief priests to hand Him over to them. ¹¹And when they heard this, they were glad and promised to give him silver. So he started looking for a good opportunity to betray Him.

The first two verses of Mark 14 establish the setting for the anointing of Jesus. Passover is quickly approaching and the population of Jerusalem has swelled from fifty thousand to two hundred fifty thousand, dramatically increasing the powder-keg atmosphere that can spark a riot. The search for a way to arrest Jesus will end in verse 10 when Judas volunteers to hand him over.

Again Mark uses his bookend device. On either side of the beautiful story of the anointing of Jesus' head are the portentous bookends of the religious officials who want him betrayed and Judas who is more than willing to do so.

We know that Jesus and the disciples have been staying in Bethany (see Mk 11:11). Is this the house of Lazarus? Is Simon the Leper their father who Jesus might have healed (Mk 14:3)? Might the woman in the story be Mary herself?[20] The time frames match. Mark's anonymous woman is almost certainly Mary.

The fact that Simon's guests are "reclining" hints that this is a formal dinner. With no introduction, with no further explanation of this setting, we are simply told that a nameless woman has broken an expensive alabaster jar filled with nard and poured the perfume over Jesus' head. It is an over-the-top, extravagant gesture. The perfume, a rare extract from a plant that grows in far-off India, is worth tens of thousands of dollars. The fact that the perfume is contained in a jar of alabaster indicates its enormous value. Breaking the jar means it will never be used again. In Mark's Gospel some unnamed guests object. Matthew tells us it is the disciples (Mt 26:8). John tells us specifically that it is Judas who objects (Jn 12:4-5).

In keeping with his tendency to stand up for the marginalized, including and especially women, Jesus defends the nameless woman. Referencing Deuteronomy 15:11, he reminds the Twelve that the opportunity to provide for the poor will always be the there. He will not.

I imagine Jesus turning to the woman as he speaks to the disciples, saying, "She has anointed My body in advance for burial" (Mk 14:8). I can see her breath being taken away by Jesus' words. She has done more than she realized. Next, Jesus does something unique. This story and its parallel in Matthew 26 contain the only reference to him doing anything remotely like it; he memorializes her gift: "Wherever the gospel is proclaimed in the whole world, what this woman has done will also be told in memory of her" (Mk 14:9). The extravagant gift of an unnamed woman who acted out more perhaps than she knew—she is being integrated into the story of the gospel! Her story has become part of his.

In contrast to the remarkable charity of the woman, Mark paints a picture of Judas leaving and going to the chief priests. The final phase of the dark bookend pictures Judas actively looking for an opportunity to hand Jesus over.

For most of my life, I've assumed it was the washing of the disciples' feet in John 13 that drove Judas over the edge and into his betrayal of Jesus. The more I look at the story of the generous woman, and the more I listen to Jesus' words memorializing her actions, the more I realize the Twelve never did anything up to that point deserving such commendation. And I think it might have been this anointing that drove Judas—jealous, deceitful Judas—to do what he finally did.

THE LORD'S SUPPER

12 On the first day of Unleavened Bread, when they sacrifice the Passover lamb, His disciples asked Him, "Where do You want us to go and prepare the Passover so You may eat it?"

13 So He sent two of His disciples and told them, "Go into the city, and a man carrying a water jug will meet you. Follow him. 14 Wherever he enters, tell the owner of the house, 'The Teacher says, "Where is the guest room for Me to eat the Passover with My disciples?"' 15 He will show you a large room upstairs, furnished and ready. Make the preparations for us there." 16 So the disciples went out, entered the city, and found it just as He had told them, and they prepared the Passover.

17 When evening came, He arrived with the Twelve. 18 While they were reclining and eating, Jesus said, "I assure you: One of you will betray Me— one who is eating with Me!"

19 They began to be distressed and to say to Him one by one, "Surely not I?"

20 He said to them, "[It is] one of the Twelve—the one who is dipping bread with Me in the bowl. 21 For the Son of Man will go just as it is written about Him, but woe to that man by whom the Son of Man is betrayed! It would have been better for that man if he had not been born."

22 As they were eating, He took bread, blessed and broke it, gave it to them, and said, "Take [it]; this is My body."

23 Then He took a cup, and after giving thanks, He gave it to them, and so they all drank from it. 24 He said to them, "This is My blood [that establishes the covenant]; it is shed for many. 25 I assure you: I will no longer drink of the fruit of the vine until that day when I drink it in a new way in the kingdom of God." 26 After singing psalms, they went out to the Mount of Olives.

*B*y our best reckoning it is Thursday night, the thirteenth of Nisan, A.D. 33. The Judean Jews will celebrate the Passover meal on Friday.

Jesus and his Galilean disciples, following the tradition begun by the Diaspora community, celebrate their feast on Thursday night. Peter leaves his name out of Mark's account, but Luke 22:8 tells us the two disciples Jesus sent ahead in Mark 14:13 were Peter and John. The prearranged signal of the man carrying the water jar reminds us of the prearrangement made for the donkey in Mark 11:2. Unless Jesus has established an intimate relationship with more than one wealthy household in the city of Jerusalem, this appears to be the same house. Chances are it is the same house mentioned in Acts 12:12. This could mean that the house where the Lord's Supper was celebrated was the home of Mark himself!

Once again we receive the detail that the Twelve are "reclining" with Jesus. This is a formal meal. Mark's account is characteristically brief. He does not tell us all he knows, but all we need to know. Jesus sets a somber tone for the evening by predicting that one of them will betray him. For the rest of the meal—indeed, for the rest of the night—the Twelve remain unsettled by Jesus' prediction. In the garden they will be "exhausted from their grief" (Lk 22:45).

In Mark's account, Judas is not directly implicated at the meal. In Matthew, Judas protests his innocence (Mt 26:25). In the Gospel of John, Jesus whispers to him that the betrayer is the one to whom he will give the bread (Jn 13:26-27). Judas will always be a dark dilemma. How can a person share three intimate years at Jesus' side, go out on successful mission in his name and yet so cold-bloodedly betray him?

In one single verse (Mk 14:22), Jesus breaks the bread, identifying it as his body. In the following two verses he passes the cup and solemnly tells them it represents his poured-out blood. According to John's Gospel, Jesus has prepared the disciples for this disturbing image early in the ministry, back in Capernaum (Jn 6:51-63). As the meal comes to a close, Jesus adapts the traditional Jewish toast "This year in Jerusalem; next year in the kingdom." He says, "I assure you: I will no longer drink of the fruit of the vine until that day when I drink it in a new way in the kingdom of God" (Mk 14:25). Mark tells us the disciples sing a song before they move out into the darkness of the Mount of Olives. It is the only time in the course of Jesus' life when we read of Jesus singing.

THE EMOTIONAL UNRAVELING OF PETER

27 Then Jesus said to them, "All of you will run away, because it is written:

I will strike the shepherd,
and the sheep will be scattered.

28 But after I have been resurrected, I will go ahead of you to Galilee."

29 Peter told Him, "Even if everyone runs away, I will certainly not!"

30 "I assure you," Jesus said to him, "today, this very night, before the rooster crows twice, you will deny Me three times!"

31 But he kept insisting, "If I have to die with You, I will never deny You!" And they all said the same thing.

What occupies three chapters in John's Gospel (Jn 15—17) Mark covers in only five verses. Before the meal Jesus said one of them would betray him. Now as they move among the shadows, he tells the Twelve that all of them will fall away, quoting Zechariah 13:7 to substantiate his prophecy. In the next breath Jesus speaks of his resurrection and of their meeting again in Galilee (see Mt 28:16; Acts 1:11). But Peter has stopped listening after the first statement about them falling away. He does not seem to have heard about Jesus rising or meeting them in Galilee. After the resurrection, the angel will make a special point to remind Peter of the Galilee appointment (see Mk 16:7).

This will be the most difficult day of Peter's life. Repeatedly he will make what he believes to be the proper assumptions: that Jesus should not wash his feet, that he will not fall away, that he will willingly die for Jesus. Each time Jesus will rebuke and correct him. When he is ready to fight with his sword he will turn and see Jesus surrender. His world will fall to pieces. But Jesus has a better world waiting. Peter's last hope will die. But a better hope will be born.

ABBA

32 Then they came to a place named Gethsemane, and He told His disciples, "Sit here while I pray." 33 He took Peter, James, and John with Him, and He began to be deeply distressed and horrified. 34 Then He said to them, "My soul is swallowed up in sorrow—to the point of death. Remain here and stay awake." ³⁵ *Then He went a little farther, fell to the ground, and began to pray that if it were possible, the hour might pass from Him.* ³⁶ *And He said, "Abba, Father! All things are possible for You. Take this cup away from Me. Nevertheless, not what I will, but what You will."*

³⁷ *Then He came and found them sleeping. "Simon, are you sleeping?" He asked Peter. "Couldn't you stay awake one hour?* ³⁸ *Stay awake and pray so that you won't enter into temptation. The spirit is willing, but the flesh is weak."*

³⁹ *Once again He went away and prayed, saying the same thing.* ⁴⁰ *And He came again and found them sleeping, because they could not keep their eyes open. They did not know what to say to Him.* ⁴¹ *Then He came a third time and said to them, "Are you still sleeping and resting? Enough! The time has come. Look, the Son of Man is being betrayed into the hands of sinners.* ⁴² *Get up; let's go! See—My betrayer is near."*

*T*he Garden of Gethsemane is located on the slope of the Mount of Olives. This is a place Jesus frequented. (Later, Judas seems certain he'll find Jesus there.) Jesus leaves eight of the disciples at the entrance, taking Peter, James and John deeper into the grove. It is their last time to be together this side of the cross. The knowledge of this, in addition to all he knows is waiting for him, is almost more than Jesus can bear— almost. He tells the three disciples that the sorrow is almost killing him. In the vast range of Mark's portrayal of the emotional life of Jesus, this moment is the most emotionally charged. While Jesus has told the eight to "sit here," he tells the three to "keep watch" (Mk 14:32-34 NIV).

Going still farther into the darkness, Jesus collapses on the ground, pleading that the hour might pass from him. He enters the garden in effect telling the Father, "If you can get me out of this, I want out!" I have heard it said that this was the one moment when Jesus fought against the Father's will, but I take his humanity more to heart. Throughout his life Jesus struggled, as you and I struggle, with conforming his will to the Father's. Clearly this moment of all the others was the most intense, the most costly.

From out of the shadows we hear Jesus' voice, speaking his own native tongue as only Mark provides for us. It is the voice of a desperate child saying "Abba." It is the infant's intimate name for the father, *Ab*, in Aramaic. At no place in the ancient literature is God referred to by that intimate name. As far as we know, Jesus is the first person to ever reach out to the Father as "Abba."[21]

Like a pleading child, Jesus cries out in emotional agony, "All things are possible for You." Then, one last desperate gasp: "Take this cup away from Me" (Mk 14:36). Between that last utterance and the next lies an eternity of time. In that endless moment, Jesus passes from the shadow of temptation into the light of victory. The small particle in Greek, *alla*, translated "nevertheless," represents volumes. "Nevertheless, not what I will, but what You will" (Mk 14:36).

It is the battle before the final war. He limps back to find the three disciples asleep. Only Peter is rebuked. "Simon, are you sleeping?" he asks, exhausted (Mk 14:37). Jesus wants Peter to be watchful and prayerful so he will not fall into temptation. Returning to pray, to ask for strength to accomplish what he has already committed himself to do, Jesus returns later to find them sleeping once more. Peter remembers that "they did not know what to say to Him" (Mk 14:40). Later, a third time Jesus comes back to find them still asleep. They are failed lookouts. Jesus sees the mob moving through the shadows with the ghostly light of their torches and lanterns darting through the trees.

THE KISS

⁴³While He was still speaking, Judas, one of the Twelve, suddenly arrived. With him was a mob, with swords and clubs, from the chief priests, the scribes, and the elders. ⁴⁴His betrayer had given them a signal. "The One I kiss," he said, "He's the One; arrest Him and take Him away under guard." ⁴⁵So when he came, he went right up to Him and said, "Rabbi!"—and kissed Him. ⁴⁶Then they took hold of Him and arrested Him. ⁴⁷And one of those who stood by drew his sword, struck the high priest's slave, and cut off his ear.

⁴⁸But Jesus said to them, "Have you come out with swords and clubs, as though I were a criminal, to capture Me? ⁴⁹Every day I was among you, teaching in the temple complex, and you didn't arrest Me. But the Scriptures must be fulfilled." [50] Then they all deserted Him and ran away.

[51] Now a certain young man, having a linen cloth wrapped around his naked body, was following Him. They caught hold of him, [52] but he left the linen cloth behind and ran away naked.

*M*ark uses his favorite word, "suddenly" (*eutheos*) to describe how Judas appears on the scene in verse 43. The armed mob is with him, along with the triple alliance of the chief priests, the scribes and the elders. We get a glimpse into the stony heart of Judas by the sign he has prearranged—a kiss, a demonstration of affection and intimacy. This is how he will single Jesus out to be arrested.

As they lay hands on Jesus, "one of those who stood by" (Mk 14:47) lashes out at one of the high priest's slaves with his sword, cutting off his ear. None of the Synoptics name the culprit. Only John, all those decades later, after Peter is safely in the grave, lets us know who wielded the sword (Jn 18:10). If Peter was still alive when Mark wrote his Gospel, he was not purposely concealing his identity. More likely it was a matter of the church's safety—it would not look good for a leader of the young, suspect church to be known as one who wielded swords. And don't think for a moment Peter was aiming at the ear. His stroke was horizontal, clipping only the "little ear," or earlobe. The fact is, he was aiming for the man's neck.

Exhausted, perhaps even bloody from his ordeal in the garden, Jesus has little patience for the religious leaders' violent hypocrisy. Had they not been cowards, they would have arrested him any time in the temple courts.

In Mark 14:51-52 we find a tantalizing possibility. Mark tells us of a "young man" wrapped only in a linen cloth who has been following Jesus. When the mob tries to seize him he spins around and runs away naked. If Mark's house was indeed the one Jesus used for the Last Supper, perhaps the young Mark knew of their intention to spend the night in the garden. In the middle of the night, hearing the mob pass by his house on their way to arrest Jesus, he leaps out of bed, hurriedly wrapping himself in a linen sheet, hoping to get to Jesus in time to warn him and the disciples of what is about to happen. Instead, arriving too late, Mark is almost caught and arrested having identified himself as being with Jesus and the Twelve. It is a glorious, fascinating and ultimately unprovable assumption!

I AM

[53] They led Jesus away to the high priest, and all the chief priests, the elders, and the scribes convened. [54] Peter followed Him at a distance, right into the high priest's courtyard. He was sitting with the temple police, warming himself by the fire.

[55] The chief priests and the whole Sanhedrin were looking for testimony against Jesus to put Him to death, but they could find none. [56] For many were giving false testimony against Him, but the testimonies did not agree. [57] Some stood up and were giving false testimony against Him, stating, [58] "We heard Him say, 'I will demolish this sanctuary made by [human] hands, and in three days I will build another not made by hands.'" [59] Yet their testimony did not agree even on this.

[60] Then the high priest stood up before them all and questioned Jesus, "Don't You have an answer to what these men are testifying against You?" [61] But He kept silent and did not answer anything. Again the high priest questioned Him, "Are You the Messiah, the Son of the Blessed One?"

[62] "I am," said Jesus, "and all of you will see the Son of Man seated at the right hand of the Power and coming with the clouds of heaven."

[63] Then the high priest tore his robes and said, "Why do we still need witnesses? [64] You have heard the blasphemy! What is your decision?"

And they all condemned Him to be deserving of death. [65] Then some began to spit on Him, to blindfold Him, and to beat Him, saying, "Prophesy!" Even the temple police took Him and slapped Him.

[66] While Peter was in the courtyard below, one of the high priest's servants came. [67] When she saw Peter warming himself, she looked at him and said, "You also were with that Nazarene, Jesus."

[68] But he denied it: "I don't know or understand what you're talking about!" Then he went out to the entryway, and a rooster crowed.

[69] When the servant saw him again she began to tell those standing nearby, "This man is one of them!"

70But again he denied it. After a little while those standing there said to Peter again, "You certainly are one of them, since you're also a Galilean!"

71Then he started to curse and to swear with an oath, "I don't know this man you're talking about!"

72Immediately a rooster crowed a second time, and Peter remembered when Jesus had spoken the word to him, "Before the rooster crows twice, you will deny Me three times." When he thought about it, he began to weep.

Only John 18:13 informs us that Jesus was held at the house of Annas while the Sanhedrin were called for their initial late-night illegal meeting. The law stipulated that the counsel was supposed to meet only in daylight hours. The same threefold alliance appears before the high priest, trying to establish a charge against Jesus. But they are unable to get their numerous false witnesses to agree. One charge they try to make stick goes all the way back to the first year of Jesus' ministry. During the first temple expulsion in John 2:19, Jesus spoke of destroying the temple and rebuilding it in three days. (It is a charge that will hound even Stephen in Acts 6:13-14.)

The high priests, whom Mark neglects to name, press Jesus to answer their charges. At first Jesus keeps silent, but when confronted directly with the question "Are you the Messiah?" he responds, "I am" (Mk 14:61-62). It is not clear whether this response is a statement of the ineffable name of God, which was not supposed to be spoken (Ex 3:14). There is a lack of agreement among scholars. Some see the response of the high priest tearing his robes as a confirmation that Jesus has spoken the name "Yahweh." Throughout Mark's Gospel, Jesus has hesitated to speak of his identity as the Messiah. This caution is seen in his numerous commands for secrecy to those he healed or otherwise revealed himself to. But now that time is over. The days of secrecy have passed. Before the supreme court of that day, Jesus confesses that they will someday see him seated at the right hand of the power (God), coming with the clouds of heaven.

With Jesus' statement as evidence, there is no longer any need for witnesses. The court passes the death sentence. For the moment the dark

triple alliance has won. As he has repeatedly prophesied, Jesus is spit
upon and beaten (see Mk 10:34). In a uniquely Jewish form of torment,
he is also blindfolded. As they are beating him they ask him to prophesy—that is, to determine who has struck him. There was a cultural
tradition at the time, based on an interpretation of Isaiah 11:3, that the
Messiah would not judge by what he saw or heard. The rabbis concluded
that the Messiah would therefore judge by his sense of smell.

Earlier we were told that Peter followed the mob at a distance and
eventually settled beside a fire in the courtyard. After the scene of the
first trial, Mark cuts back to Peter in verse 66. It is the bookend device
once more. On either side of the story of Jesus making his confession
before the high priest we find the story of Peter's denials. The first
person to confront Peter is a female slave. All four Gospels agree that
Peter's first accuser is a woman. We learn in the fourth Gospel that
John speaks to the serving girl in order for Peter to be let into the courtyard (Jn 18:15-16). Even without that detail, Mark reports that she
confronts Peter with the words, "You also were with him." As Peter
tries to escape to the entryway he hears the first rooster crow.

Mark goes on to tell how the girl stirs up the crowd by telling them,
"This man is one of them!" (Mk 14:69). Apparently John is too young
to be seen as a threat by the crowd. After some longer period of time,
Peter's Galilean accent gives him away. When the crowd confronts
him, Peter begins to swear, making an oath that he does not know the
man they are talking about. At that moment, the rooster crows a second time. Remembering Jesus' words, Peter breaks down in tears.

Two of Jesus' disciples betrayed him that night. One wept and eventually found forgiveness. The other tried with his own devices to fix the
mess he had made and ended up at the end of a rope.

MARK 15

BEFORE PILATE

15:1–15 The Roman trial begins.

JESUS CRUCIFIED

15:16–32 The soldiers place him on the cross.

THE TORN CURTAIN

15:33–41 The death of Jesus.

A RICH MAN OF COURAGE

15:42–47 Joseph claims Jesus' corpse.

BEFORE PILATE

¹As soon as it was morning, the chief priests had a meeting with the elders, scribes, and the whole Sanhedrin. After tying Jesus up, they led Him away and handed Him over to Pilate.

²So Pilate asked Him, "Are You the King of the Jews?"

He answered him, "You have said it."

³And the chief priests began to accuse Him of many things. ⁴Then Pilate questioned Him again, "Are You not answering anything? Look how many things they are accusing You of!" ⁵But Jesus still did not answer anything, so Pilate was amazed.

⁶At the festival it was Pilate's custom to release for the people a prisoner they requested. ⁷There was one named Barabbas, who was in prison with rebels who had committed murder during the rebellion. ⁸The crowd came up and began to ask [Pilate] to do for them as was his custom. ⁹So Pilate answered them, "Do you want me to release the King of the Jews for you?" ¹⁰For he knew it was because of envy that the chief priests had handed Him over. ¹¹But the chief priests stirred up the crowd so that he would release Barabbas to them instead.

¹²Pilate asked them again, "Then what do you want me to do with the One you call the King of the Jews?"

¹³Again they shouted, "Crucify Him!"

¹⁴Then Pilate said to them, "Why? What has He done wrong?"

But they shouted, "Crucify Him!" all the more.

¹⁵Then, willing to gratify the crowd, Pilate released Barabbas to them. And after having Jesus flogged, he handed Him over to be crucified.

The threefold alliance of religious leaders has come to understand the habits of Roman officials. They know the Romans get their business done early in the morning so the rest of their day can be spent in "organized leisure." So they reach a decision. They will translate their charge of blasphemy (which no Roman official would recognize) into a civil charge of treason. The governor will be forced to deal with such a charge or become subject to charges from Rome himself.

We know a lot about Pontius Pilate. Even secular historians such as

Philo of Alexandria paint a negative portrait of him.[22] He was assigned to be a prefect (military commander) of the region in A.D. 26. Though his residence was on the coast of the Mediterranean, at Caesarea in one of Herod's empty palaces, Pilate came to Jerusalem to be in residence during the festivals, when trouble was most likely to occur.

The most important piece of background in understanding Pilate's mindset is how he obtained his position—or, more to the point, through whom he obtained it. His name was Aelius Sejanus. Next to Tiberius himself, he was the most powerful man in Rome. In A.D. 31 he was appointed consul, virtually a co-ruler with the emperor. On October 18 of that same year, it was discovered that he had been plotting against Tiberius, planning a takeover. Within hours he was executed. Sejanus had been well-known for his anti-Semitic policies, and upon his death Tiberius ordered, "Hostilities against the Jews will cease."[23] This is a vital piece of the puzzle for understanding Pilate.

Pilate is now standing before the most influential men in Jerusalem. He loathes them and all they stand for. He sees through their duplicity and jealousy. Yet in order to keep his position, he must be seen as unbiased and fair, otherwise he will come under the scrutiny of Tiberius, a scrutiny that has increased exponentially since the Sejanus affair. Pilate would in fact be recalled to Rome in A.D. 36 to answer for atrocities committed against the Samaritans. While he was on his way to stand trial, Tiberius died and Pilate simply disappeared.[24]

This is the powerful, twisted man who confronts the bound Jesus with the question, "Are You the king of the Jews?" (Mk 15:2). Then come the only words Jesus speaks to Pilate in the Synoptics: "You have said it." (John 18 provides a more detailed account of their conversation.) This is not the answer Pilate is looking for. He wants this ripple in his day to be over as soon as possible. He is still hoping he can make it to the baths.

The "many things" the chief priests are accusing Jesus of include inciting riots, opposing taxes and claiming to be a king (see Lk 23:2). Jesus' failure to answer only increases the governor's irritation. In fact, his behavior becomes the pattern and paradigm for Mark's readers, who will soon be standing before Roman officials themselves, being confronted with more false witnesses and bogus charges.

Mark omits the second part of the Roman trial, when Jesus is sent to Herod Antipas (see Lk 23:6). This is consistent with Mark's method of not telling us everything he knows, only what we need to know.

Releasing a criminal during Passover must have been Pilate's private custom. It is mentioned nowhere else in the ancient literature. A man ironically named "the son of the father," Barabbas, is a convicted murder and insurrectionist and the other choice for being freed. Is this Pilate's way of galling the chief priests, giving them a totally unacceptable alternative to Jesus? Is he forcing them to choose to let Jesus go? "Surely," he thinks to himself, "they would never choose Barabbas." He would eventually cause more trouble for the Jews than the harmless Nazarene carpenter.

The crowd—or, more properly, the rabble of Jerusalem—is completely under the control of the priests. It is not difficult to incite them to cry out for Barabbas to be released and Jesus crucified. As obscure as his motives might have been before, Pilate's language is now clearly inflammatory. A Roman official yields to the influence of the mob and hands over an innocent man for crucifixion while a convicted murderer is set free. It is a familiar-sounding exchange.

It was the custom to flog criminals before crucifying them; the shock and blood loss would hasten death on the cross. If we take into account John 19:1, Jesus might have been flogged twice, though the chances of surviving two Roman floggings are slim. When movies portray Jesus receiving thirty-nine stripes, they are incorrect. Thirty-nine stripes was part of Jewish synagogue discipline and was administered with rods (2 Cor 11:24). However, it was the Romans who flogged Jesus. They utilized not rods but the gruesome flagellum, a collection of heavy leather straps set with pieces of bone, glass and lead weights. There was no stipulation about how many lashes a convict might receive. The only reference in first-century literature says that a man would be flogged until the flesh hung from his back. People were frequently disemboweled by the flagellum. It could tear through the flesh and bite into bone and sinews. Josephus refers to a scourging he witnessed that resulted in the entrails of the victim becoming visible.[25]

Mark's Roman readers would have been all too familiar with seeing innocent friends tied to a pillar to receive a Roman scourging. While the image would have been alive in their imaginations, it is difficult for us to engage fully with such unimaginable cruelty and pain. Yet engage we must if we are to begin to appreciate the price Jesus paid to purchase us as his servants.

JESUS CRUCIFIED

16 Then the soldiers led Him away into the courtyard (that is, headquarters) and called the whole company together. 17 They dressed Him in a purple robe, twisted together a crown of thorns, and put it on Him. 18 And they began to salute Him, "Hail, King of the Jews!" 19 They kept hitting Him on the head with a reed and spitting on Him. Getting down on their knees, they were paying Him homage.

20 When they had mocked Him, they stripped Him of the purple robe, put His clothes on Him, and led Him out to crucify Him.

21 They forced a man coming in from the country, who was passing by, to carry Jesus' cross. He was Simon, a Cyrenian, the father of Alexander and Rufus. 22 And they brought Jesus to the place called Golgotha *(which means Skull Place). 23 They tried to give Him wine mixed with myrrh, but He did not take it. 24 Then they crucified Him and divided His clothes, casting lots for them to decide what each would get. 25 Now it was nine in the morning when they crucified Him. 26 The inscription of the charge written against Him was:*

THE KING OF THE JEWS

27 They crucified two criminals with Him, one on His right and one on His left. 28 [So the Scripture was fulfilled that says: And He was counted among outlaws.] 29 Those who passed by were yelling insults at Him, shaking their heads, and saying, "Ha! The One who would demolish the sanctuary and build it in three days, 30 save Yourself by coming down from the cross!" 31 In the same way, the chief priests with the scribes were mocking Him to one another and saying, "He saved others; He cannot save Himself! 32 Let the Messiah, the King of Israel, come down now from the cross, so that we may see and believe." Even those who were crucified with Him were taunting Him.

*J*esus is led into the praetor's residence, known as the Praetorium. Its location is still open to question. It might have been Herod's palace, close to the Tower of David. Many scholars believe it was located in the Antonia fortress, which overlooked the temple courts.

The Roman soldiers we meet in Jerusalem are not from Palestine. They are members of the Italian cohort (see Acts 10:1). By far the majority of references to the relationship between Roman soldiers and Jewish citizens are negative. The two groups were constantly antagonizing each other. The soldiers had great disdain for Jewish customs and sensibilities. Riots were frequently caused by their insensitivity to the many prohibitions of Jewish culture.

To the soldiers, tormenting Jesus is merely an event to break up the monotony of their day. Having heard the charges, they torture him according to a popular board game from the ancient world known as "Kings." Pavement stones from all over the empire still display the checkerboard design upon which the game was played, scratched into the stones by soldiers who were on duty. A piece was moved around the board according to the roll of the dice. At various stages it was robed, then crowned and finally, when it arrived at the proper square, the winner would declare "King!" As Jesus becomes their plaything, the soldiers robe him with one of their red military cloaks designed to hide any telltale signs of blood. Next they crown him. Roman emperors wore "vegetative" crowns of laurel or withered celery. The cruel crown fashioned by these soldiers is a leafy one as well, only it contains thorns. The custom was that crucified criminals would be stripped naked on the cross. For now, Mark tells us, the soldiers put Jesus' clothes back on him as they herd him to the place of crucifixion.

It is often assumed that Jesus stumbled under the weight of the cross beam he was forced to carry. But there's no word of this in the Gospels. Along the way the soldiers take advantage of a Roman law that allows them to "impress" anyone, forcing them to carry a burden for the stipulated distance of one mile (see Mt 5:41). If our ears are sensitively tuned to Mark's Gospel, at this point we should be startled to hear the personal name of someone from the crowd. Mark, normally reluctant to name names, introduces Simon of Cyrene into the narrative. Simon was probably a member of the Cyrenean synagogue in Jerusalem, whose members will come into conflict with Stephen in Acts 6:9. We are also given the names of his two sons, Rufus and Alexander. Mark almost certainly mentions them because they were known to the first readers of his Gospel. In Romans 16:13, in the midst of a long list of greetings, Paul refers to a man named Rufus. If we are correct that Mark is writing his Gospel to the Christians in Rome, chances are good that the Rufus Paul greets is the same Rufus whose father carried the cross for Jesus. It is a fascinating though uncertain connection.

The party of eight—four soldiers (Jn 19:23), two previously condemned criminals, and Jesus and Simon—finally reach Golgotha. They are accompanied by the crowd, which contains the faithful women, at least one disciple (the young John), and a number of chief priests and scribes. The precise location is hotly debated. Golgotha is derived from the Hebrew word for "skull," *gulgolet*. The Latin word for "skull," *calvaria*, is the source for the name Calvary. When they reach the place of execution, Jesus is offered drugged wine. This wine, which Matthew says Jesus tasted but refused, was offered by the pious women of Jerusalem to criminals as an act of mercy to ease their pain. The custom was based on a passage from Proverbs:

> Give beer to anyone who is dying,
> and wine to one whose life is bitter.
>
> Let him drink so that he can forget his poverty
> and remember his trouble no more. (Prov 31:6-7)

Jesus has vowed not to drink wine until he can do so with his disciples in the kingdom (Mk 14:25). He will not go to the cross with his senses dulled by drugs.

All the Gospels are minimalist in describing the crucifixion. There is no word of Jesus' hands and feet being nailed, only "Then they crucified him" (Mk 15:24). Mark's readers needed no gory details. A cross with the rotting corpse of a slave was a common sight in the countryside of the Roman Empire. Nero would crucify Christians in his garden and set them on fire in the night as human torches. The agony of the cross is preserved for us in the English word "excruciating." It is apparent that Jesus is now naked. The soldiers have taken his clothes and are casting lots to see who will win them (see Ps 22:18).

There are problems reconciling the exact hour of Jesus' crucifixion. John 19:14 places it at "about six in the morning." But by Mark's reference to "nine in the morning" (Mk 15:25), it appears Jesus was on the cross from that time until three in the afternoon (Mk 15:33). For the last three hours the cross was shrouded in darkness.

The charge against Jesus is painted, perhaps on a wooden plank coated with white gypsum. Mark's version of the charge is the shortest, simply "THE KING OF THE JEWS" (Mk 15:26). Matthew tells us that the plaque is hung above Jesus' head (Mt 27:37). All of the Gospels indicate that the two criminals are crucified on either side of him, with Jesus hanging in the center. The earlier charge, that he would destroy the temple, is taken up in the mockery of the crowd.

In Mark 15:31 we are told that the religious leaders join in with the crowd taunting Jesus. In verse 32 the criminals who share his grim fate also heap insults on Jesus. He is completely cut off, alone, comfortless. His disciples have denied him and fled. His other followers are nowhere to be found. In the distance, we are told, the women who care for him are watching (Mk 15:40). For three hours Jesus endures mockery and insults. At noon the scene dramatically shifts.

THE TORN CURTAIN

33 When it was noon, darkness came over the whole land until three in the afternoon. 34 And at three Jesus cried out with a loud voice, "Eloi, Eloi, lemá sabachtháni?" which is translated, "My God, My God, why have You forsaken Me?"

35 When some of those standing there heard this, they said, "Look, He's calling for Elijah!" 36 Someone ran and filled a sponge with sour wine, fixed it on a reed, offered Him a drink, and said, "Let's see if Elijah comes to take Him down!"

37 But Jesus let out a loud cry and breathed His last. 38 Then the curtain of the sanctuary was split in two from top to bottom. 39 When the centurion, who was standing opposite Him, saw the way He breathed His last, he said, "This man really was God's Son!"

⁴⁰There were also women looking on from a distance. Among them were Mary Magdalene, Mary the mother of James the younger and of Joses, and Salome. ⁴¹When He was in Galilee, they would follow Him and help Him. Many other women had come up with Him to Jerusalem.

I tend to imagine the three hours of darkness at Golgotha as having been the result of a terrific storm. At least that is how it is portrayed in the Jesus movies. But read the text clearly. There's no word of thunder or lightning in any of the Gospels, only of darkness. I've come to imagine a more terrifying experience than thunder and lightning: absolute stillness. The three ominous hours of darkness accompanied by an ominous silence over Jerusalem. The prophet Amos describes the darkness like this:

> I will make the sun go down at noon;
> I will darken the land in the daytime.
> I will turn your feasts into mourning. . . .
> I will make that grief
> like mourning for an only son. (Amos 8:9-11)

Abraham experienced the terror of this darkness in Genesis 15:12. Once the Lord had blown the noisy locusts away from Egypt, he sent the plague of darkness, "a darkness that can be felt" (Ex 10:21). In the Old Testament this deep darkness was indicative of the presence of God (see Ex 14:20; 20:21). When Jesus hangs on the cross, God is somehow separated from him (Hab 1:13). His cry in Mark 15:34 confirms it. The silent, deep darkness points to the possibility that God's presence is hovering; perhaps his back is turned. Though we have heard God's voice twice in Mark's Gospel (Mk 1:9; 9:7), he is now silent. It may have been the most severe part of Jesus' suffering.

Jesus calls out in his own native Aramaic the words of Psalm 22:1 as the three hours of suffering in the dark come to a close. He is not delirious or confused. God forsakes him when he becomes sin for us. Hell is a price to pay for sin, and God hiding his face is hell.

Someone in the crowd confuses "eloi" for "eliya," or Elijah. It is a logical mistake. Malachi 4:3 associates the coming of the Messiah with the prophet Elijah. Jesus has just recently seen him at his transfiguration (Mk 9:4). But Elijah is not coming. No one is coming.

John tells us Jesus asks for something to drink (Jn 19:28). Here in Mark's Gospel, someone fills a sponge with sour wine and offers it to him. This is simply wine vinegar, wine that has gone bad. It was given to soldiers in the field. (Sponges were commonly used in place of toilet paper.) The detail that the sponge is placed on a stick points to Jesus being crucified on a high cross. It is all in fulfillment of Psalm 69:21. (In fact, this would be a good moment to read Psalm 69.)

Both Mark and Matthew tell us Jesus died with a loud cry. The Roman centurion, who would have been assigned the role of overseeing the crucifixion, had doubtless seen hundreds of men die on the cross, perhaps even thousands. He had never seen anyone die like this, with a shout and not a whimper or a groan.

Do not miss this moment. Along with Peter's confession in Mark 8:29, this is the other climax of Mark's Gospel. Stop and take time to engage with the text at the level of your imagination. Imagine the centurion covered in the blood of three men, a hardened warrior of the Italian cohort far from his home. "Son of God" is a title that belongs solely to the emperor he has sworn to serve. Imagine the response of Mark's first Roman readers as they hear this glorious confession coming from the lips of a Roman soldier: "Surely this man was the Son of God!" (Mk 15:39 NIV).

The soldier made it into the legends of the early church. John Wayne even played him on the silver screen. If he left a fingerprint anywhere at all, I believe it is in John's Gospel. Buried in the crucifixion account is a statement apparently made by one of the soldiers who pierced Jesus' side: "He who saw this has testified so that you also may believe. His testimony is true, and he knows he is telling the truth" (Jn 19:35).

At the moment of the centurion's confession, all the Synoptics tell of a curtain in the temple being torn from top to bottom. None of the Gospels tell us which curtain it was; there were two. The first was an outer curtain that separated the court from the sanctuary (Ex 30:36; 38:18). This would have been the most visible curtain and is perhaps the most likely choice. More people would have witnessed the tearing of this curtain. The second curtain hung between the Holy Place and the Holy of Holies (Ex 26:31-35; Lev 16:2). Only a priest would have witnessed this curtain being torn. For symbolic reasons this seems to me the better choice of the two. Because of Jesus' death, the barrier between the presence of God (which had once resided in the Holy of Holies) and all of us has been torn in two. Because of the cross, we have complete access to the Father (see Heb 6:19; 9:2-3, 6-12; 10:19-20).

In Mark 15:40-41 we meet the women who will be so crucial to the rest of Mark's story. They watch from a discreet distance. They are the feminine "three": Mary Magdalene, Mary the mother of James and Joses, and Salome. They will witness the death, burial and resurrection, the disciples having forfeited the privilege by running away. Even as they linger here in the text, we too should linger with them for a few moments. They left everything to follow Jesus. In leaving all, they have possibly lost everything. To enter into their mindset, we have to realize that for them, everything is simply over. All their hope has died with Jesus. None of the women, nor any of Jesus' disciples, will display the least hint whatsoever that they expect him to rise from the dead as he has promised. These women will go to the tomb to anoint a dead body. For them all is lost. It is over.

A RICH MAN OF COURAGE

⁴²When it was already evening, because it was preparation day (that is, the day before the Sabbath), ⁴³Joseph of Arimathea, a prominent member of the Sanhedrin who was himself looking forward to the kingdom of God, came and boldly went in to Pilate and asked for Jesus' body. ⁴⁴Pilate was surprised that He was already dead. Summoning the centurion, he asked him whether He had already died. ⁴⁵When he found out from the centurion, he gave the corpse to Joseph. ⁴⁶After he bought some fine linen, he took Him down and wrapped Him in the linen. Then he placed Him in a tomb cut out of the rock, and rolled a stone against the entrance to the tomb. ⁴⁷Now Mary Magdalene and Mary the mother of Joses were watching where He was placed.

On Friday afternoon, Joseph of Arimathea appears on the scene. John tells us he is a secret disciple of Jesus (Jn 19:38). Mark tells us he has come "boldly" to claim the body of Jesus. Joseph is a wealthy, prominent person, a member of the Sanhedrin. For him to claim Jesus' body is to identify himself with the crucified criminal. According to the Romans, those who have been crucified should be denied burial.[26]

With his position and authority, Joseph is able to come and go as he pleases. His actions might have been interpreted as the acts of a pious man. To bury the dead was the greatest act of *hesed*, or mercy, in Judaism. It was considered especially pious because the person who performed the act of burial could not be thanked.

Joseph is granted permission by Pilate, whose only surprise is that Jesus is already dead. In John 19:31-33, we learn that the other two criminals crucified with Jesus are still alive. The soldiers have to break their legs to hasten their deaths. Crucifixion normally took two to three days. One source refers to someone surviving eight days on a cross. Jesus' death in only six hours is extraordinary.

Joseph takes the body down from the cross and wraps it in linen, placing it in his own tomb (Mt 27:60). John says a man named Nicodemus helped him (Jn 19:39). Together they roll the heavy circular stone into its slot in front of the tomb. But take notice: There they are again, the two Marys, witnessing where the body is laid.

MARK 16

THEY WERE AFRAID

16:1–8 The resurrection.

THEY WERE AFRAID

¹When the Sabbath was over, Mary Magdalene, Mary the mother of James, and Salome bought spices, so they could go and anoint Him. ²Very early in the morning, on the first day of the week, they went to the tomb at sunrise. ³They were saying to one another, "Who will roll away the stone from the entrance to the tomb for us?" ⁴Looking up, they observed that the stone— which was very large—had been rolled away. ⁵When they entered the tomb they saw a young man dressed in a long white robe sitting on the right side; they were amazed and alarmed.

⁶"Don't be alarmed," he told them. "You are looking for Jesus the Naza- rene, who was crucified. He has been resurrected! He is not here! See the place where they put Him. ⁷But go, tell His disciples and Peter, 'He is going ahead of you to Galilee; you will see Him there just as He told you.'"

⁸So they went out and started running from the tomb, because trembling and astonishment overwhelmed them. And they said nothing to anyone, since they were afraid.

*I*t is early Sunday morning. The feminine three who observed Jesus' death from a distance, who stood by as Joseph and Nicodemus placed the lifeless body in the tomb, have come to perform one final act of kindness for which they do not expect thanks. Perhaps they are hoping a proper burial will restore some of the dignity that has been so vio- lently stripped from their master.

It is vital to recognize the presupposition behind the fact that they are carrying spices—they are coming to anoint a dead body. They have absolutely no expectation that Jesus will rise from the dead. It is almost as if he had never spoken of it.

The Judaism of Jesus' day observed a two-stage burial. First the body would be placed in a tomb for approximately a year. After the process of decomposition had erased the flesh, the bones would be gathered, washed and placed in an ossuary. The body was anointed only to con- trol the smell of decomposition. Jesus, they thought, had already been dead for some forty hours and would have begun to smell.

In the early morning light, as they slowly make their way to Joseph's tomb, their question betrays the absence of expectation. To ask who will roll the stone away is to presuppose that Jesus is still dead inside. The women do not seem to know that the tomb was sealed and is supposed to be under guard (Mt 27:62-66). Neither does it appear they are aware of the earthquake caused by the descending angel who rolled back the stone (Mt 28:2). But when they arrive at the tomb, the heavy stone is out of place, rolled away.

When they enter through the small doorway, they see a young man in white. They hear the words we typically hear from angels: "Don't be alarmed" (Mk 16:6). He knows why they have come. He understands what they do not know, or perhaps refuse to believe. Jesus is risen! There is nothing to hide. He invites them to examine the emptiness of the place where Jesus had lain. They are the witnesses. They need to see.

The feminine three, the faithful witnesses, are given a commission by the angel to notify Jesus' disciples of what has happened. They are entrusted with the most momentous message that would ever be spoken for one human being to another: "He has risen!" (Mk 16:6 NIV).

The words "and Peter" could not be more significant (Mk 16:6). Peter was convinced that he forfeited his right to be Jesus' disciple. The message of the angel says otherwise. The first resurrection appearance will be to Peter, though none of the Gospels record the details of the meeting (Lk 24:34; 1 Cor 15:5). Only Mark's Gospel tells of the specific angelic outreach to Peter. It would have been something he would never forget.

In Mark 14:28, Jesus told the disciples he would go ahead to meet them back in the familiarity of their home in Galilee (see Mt 28:16). He is waiting for them—at home.

We need to linger with the women in Mark 16:8. Their experience, so close to the resurrection, is nothing like ours. We tend to be joyful and confident. They are trembling, overwhelmed. They flee from the tomb. It is the same verb Mark uses to describe the disciples fleeing in fear in Mark 14:50. They revert back to what they know. Had not Jesus again and again told them to keep quiet, to maintain the secret of who he was?

Their senses overloaded, the faithful women flee in fear. And you and I are left standing beside an empty tomb, forced to decide how we will respond. Mark's final scene would have connected powerfully with his first Roman readers, whose faith, like ours, was often mixed with fear.

This momentous moment is where Mark chooses to end his Gospel. Later generations were disturbed by this seemingly abrupt ending and edited together bits and pieces of the other Gospels into what they considered a more appropriate conclusion. (For an explanation of the different later additions to the conclusion of Mark's Gospel, refer to appendix E.)

However, the abruptness of the original ending clearly fits Mark's literary style, given to a sense of immediacy. In order to appreciate the perfection of this original ending, we need to engage with our imaginations one more time.

The scene outside the tomb with the women fleeing in fear and amazement is the single moment that links the first followers of Jesus, who had actually seen and heard him, with you and me. Mark means for us to share in the emotionality of this final scene. In a sense, every other moment had been leading up to this one. It is the supreme moment, like others earlier, where believing comes *before* seeing and faith is born *before* the appearance of the proof:

- Like the moment *before* the proof of the healing of his daughter, when Jesus whispered to her father, "Don't be afraid, only believe" (Mk 5:36)

- Like the moment of Peter's great confession of belief in Jesus which, of necessity, had to come *before* the proof provided by the transfiguration (Mk 8:27–9:13)

- Like the moment when the desperate father, *before* his son was healed, cried out to Jesus, "I believe . . ." (Mk 9:24)

- *Unlike* the moment when, standing before the cross of Jesus, the priests and scribes faithlessly jeered, "Let the Messiah, the King of Israel, come down now from the cross, so that we may see and believe" (see Mk 15:32)

There is a luminous moment when belief and trust are given before the light of proof shines. Indeed, proof matters and will sometimes come, but Jesus demands that we believe before the proof (Mk 8:11-12).

So this is the moment to which Mark has brought us, at which Mark leaves us. As the three astonished women flee from the empty tomb, not having yet seen Jesus, they remember his frequent admonishment not to tell. They take to their heels, in obedience to the angel, to go and tell the disciples.

Though it is frequently used as a metaphor for the resurrection, the empty tomb is not the final proof; it is only a piece of evidence. Someone might have stolen the body, as the women had feared. Only Jesus is the final proof. And, offstage in Mark's Gospel, he is waiting for them.

When at last, exhausted, they come to the cowering disciples, the women will be privileged to speak for the first time those words on which the faith of millions is founded: "He is risen!" Like Peter's confession, which Jesus said the church is founded on, the women's words were spoken before the final proof. By not recording those words himself, Mark corners us, he leaves us out of breath, running beside the women, perhaps trying to keep up with them. He hopes we too will be left trembling and astonished at having read his testimony of Jesus Christ, the Son of God.

The abrupt ending, which intends to leave us in the place of believing without seeing, reflects Mark's original witness and father in the faith, Simon Peter. I close with his words, spoken to us today. They are his invitation to continue to engage with our imaginations:

> You love Him, though you have not seen Him. And though not seeing Him now, you believe in Him and rejoice with inexpressible and glorious joy. (1 Pet 1:8)

APPENDIX A

Ancient Sources on the Relationship Between Peter and Mark

EUSEBIUS (A.D. 260-339)

"Hot on the heels in the same reign of Claudius, a gracious Providence brought to Rome the great and mighty Peter, chosen for his merits a leader of the other apostles. Like a noble captain of God, he proclaimed the Gospel of Light and the Word that saves souls. . . . Peter's hearers, not satisfied with a single hearing or with the unwritten teaching of the divine message, pleaded with Mark, whose Gospel we have, to leave them a written summary of the teaching given them verbally, since he was a follower of Peter" (Eusebius *Apostles* 2.14).

EUSEBIUS QUOTING PAPIAS (A.D. 103)

"Mark . . . became Peter's interpreter and wrote down accurately, but not in order, all that he remembered of the things said and done by the Lord. For he had not heard the Lord or been one of His followers, but later, as I said, a follower of Peter. Peter used to teach as occasion demanded, without giving systematic arrangement to the Lord's sayings, so that Mark did not err in writing down some things just as he recalled them. For he had one overriding purpose; to omit nothing that he had heard and to make no false statements in his account" (Eusebius *Missions and Persecutions* 3.39).

EUSEBIUS QUOTING IRENAEUS (A.D. 140-202)

"After their deaths, Mark too, the disciple and interpreter of Peter, handed on to us in writing the things proclaimed by Peter" (Eusebius *Irenaeus on Holy Scripture* 5.8).

CLEMENT OF ALEXANDRIA (A.D. 150-216) QUOTING EUSEBIUS

"When Peter preached the Word publicly at Rome, and declared the Gospel by the Spirit, many who were present requested that Mark, who had been for a long time his follower and who remembered his sayings, should write down what had been proclaimed. Having composed the gospel, he gave it to those who had requested it. When Peter learned of this, he did not positively forbid it, but neither did he encourage it" (Clement of Alexandria, 6.14, quoting Eusebius, *Church History*, p. 218).

APPENDIX B

References to the Emotional Life of Jesus in the Gospels

IN MARK

1. Mark 1:25, "Jesus rebuked him."
2. Mark 1:41, "Moved with compassion, Jesus . . ."
3. Mark 1:43, "He sternly warned him."
4. Mark 3:5, "After looking around at them with anger and sorrow . . ."
5. Mark 3:12, "He would strongly warn them."
6. Mark 5:43, "He gave them strict orders."
7. Mark 6:6, "He was amazed."
8. Mark 6:34, "He . . . had compassion on them."
9. Mark 7:34, "He sighed deeply."
10. Mark 8:2, "I have compassion."
11. Mark 8:12, "Sighing deeply in His spirit, He said . . ."
12. Mark 8:30, "He strictly warned them."
13. Mark 8:32, "He was openly talking."
14. Mark 8:33, "He rebuked Peter."
15. Mark 10:14, "He was indignant."
16. Mark 14:34, "My soul is swallowed up in sorrow."

IN MATTHEW

1. Matthew 8:10, "Jesus was amazed."
2. Matthew 9:36, "He felt compassion for them."
3. Matthew 14:14, "He . . . felt compassion for them."
4. Matthew 15:32, "'I have compassion on the crowd.'"

5. Matthew 20:34, "Moved with compassion, Jesus . . ."
6. Matthew 26:37-38, "He began to be sorrowful and deeply distressed. . . . 'My soul is swallowed up in sorrow—to the point of death.'"

IN LUKE

1. Luke 4:35, "Jesus rebuked him."
2. Luke 7:9, "Jesus . . . was amazed."
3. Luke 7:13, "He had compassion on her."
4. Luke 9:21, "He strictly warned . . . them."
5. Luke 9:51, "He determined to journey to Jerusalem." (The King James Version says Jesus "set his face" to go to Jerusalem.)
6. Luke 10:21, "He rejoiced in the Holy Spirit."
7. Luke 22:44, "Being in anguish, He prayed."

IN JOHN

1. John 4:6, "Jesus, worn out from His journey . . ."
2. John 11:33, "He was angry in His spirit and deeply moved."
3. John 12:27, "Now My soul is troubled."
4. John 13:21, "He was troubled in His spirit."

APPENDIX C

Historical References to the Period of Mark's Gospel

PLINY THE YOUNGER

On the persecution of Christians

"This is the approach I have followed with those who have been brought before me on the charge of being Christians. I have asked them whether they are Christians. If they admitted it, I asked them a second and third time, with the warning of the punishment. Those who persist I command to be taken off to execution. . . . Those who deny that they are or have been Christians I lead in reciting a prayer to the gods; then, with offerings of incense and wine, they pray to your statue and in addition, speak evil of Christ. . . . Others, who were identified by an informer, declared themselves to be Christians but then denied it. They had been Christians, they said, but had ceased to be, three or more years ago—some as long as 20 years. All of these worshiped your statue and the images of the gods and reviled Christ" (Pliny *Letters* 10.96).

SUETONIUS

On the persecution of Christians in Rome under Claudius

"Because the Jews at Rome caused continuous disturbances at the instigation of Chrestus, he expelled them from the city" (Suetonius *Twelve Caesars* 25.4). Note: In Acts 18:1-3 Paul meets Priscilla and Aquila, who have recently come from Rome after being expelled by Claudius.

On the persecution of Christians in Rome under Nero

"Punishments were also inflicted on the Christians, a sect professing a new and mischievous belief" (Suetonius *Twelve Caesars* 16.2).

On Vespasian healing with spit

"As he sat at the Tribunal, two labourers, one blind, the other lame, approached together, begging to be healed. Apparently the god Serapis had promised them in a dream that if Vespasian would consent to spit in the blind man's eyes, and touch the lame man's leg with his heel, both would be made well. Vespasian had so little faith in his curative powers that he showed great reluctance in doing as he was asked; but his friends persuaded him to try them, in the presence of a large audience, too—and the charm worked" (Suetonius *Twelve Caesars* 10.7).

TACITUS
On the persecution of Christians in Rome after the fire

"To suppress the rumor, Nero fabricated scapegoats—and punished with every refinement the notoriously depraved Christians (as they were popularly called). Their originator, Christ, had been executed in Tiberius' reign by the governor of Judaea, Pontius Pilate. But in spite of this temporary setback the deadly superstition had broken out afresh, not only in Judaea (where the mischief had started) but even in Rome. All degraded and shameful practices collect and flourish in the capital.

"First, Nero had self-acknowledged Christians arrested. Then, on their information, large numbers of others were condemned—not so much for incendiarism as for their anti-social tendencies. Their deaths were made farcical. Dressed in wild animals' skins, they were torn to pieces by dogs, or crucified, or made into torches to be ignited after dark as substitutes for daylight. Nero provided his gardens for the spectacle, and exhibited displays in the Circus, at which he mingled with the crowd—or stood in a chariot, dressed as a charioteer. Despite their guilt as Christians, and the ruthless punishment it deserved, the victims were pitied. For it was felt that they were being sacrificed to one man's brutality rather than to the national interest" (Tacitus *Annals of Rome* 15.44).

JOSEPHUS

On the death of John the Baptist

"Now some of the Jews thought that the destruction of Herod's army came from God, and that very justly, as a punishment of what he did against John, that was called the Baptist: for Herod slew him, who was a good man, and commanded the Jews to exercise virtue, both as to righteousness toward one another, and piety toward God, and so to come to baptism; for that the washing [with water] would be acceptable to him, if they made use of it, not in order to the putting away [or the remission] of some sins [only], but for the purification of the body; supposing still that the soul was thoroughly purified beforehand by righteousness. Now when [many] others came in crowds about him, for they were very greatly moved [or pleased] by hearing his words, Herod, who feared lest the great influence John had over the people might put it into his power and inclination to raise a rebellion (for they seemed ready to do any thing he should advise), thought it best, by putting him to death, to prevent any mischief he might cause, and not bring himself into difficulties, by sparing a man who might make him repent of it when it would be too late. Accordingly he was sent a prisoner, out of Herod's suspicious temper, to Macherus, the castle I before mentioned, and was there put to death. Now the Jews had an opinion that the destruction of this army was sent as a punishment upon Herod, and a mark of God's displeasure to him" (Josephus *Antiquities* 18.5.2).

On the temple

"Now the temple was built of stones that were white and strong, and each of their length was twenty-five cubits, their height was at eight and their breadth about twelve; and the whole structure, as also the structure of the royal cloister, was on each side much lower, but the middle was much higher, till they were visible to those that dwelt in the country for a great many furlongs, but chiefly to such as lived over against them, and those that approach them. The temple had doors also at the entrance, and lintels over them, of the same height with a temple in itself. They were a door and with embroidered veils, with their flowers of purple, and pillars interwoven: and over these, but under the crown-work, was spread out a golden vine, with its branches hanging down from a great height, the largeness and fine workmanship of which was a surprising sight to the spectators, to see what the vast materials there were, and with what great skill the workmanship was done. He also encompassed the entire temple with very large cloisters, contriving them to be in a due proportion thereto; and he laid out larger sums of money upon them than had been done before him, till it seemed that no one else had so greatly adorned the temple as he had done. There was a large wall to both the cloisters; which wall was in itself the most prodigious work that was ever heard of by man" (Josephus *Antiquities* 15.11.3).

"Now the outward face of the temple in its front wanted nothing that was likely to surprise either men's minds or their eyes: for it was covered all over with plates of gold of great weight, and, at the first rising of the sun, reflected back a very fiery splendor, and made those who forced themselves to look upon it to turn their eyes away, just as they would have done at the Sun's own rays. But this temple appeared to strangers, when they were at a distance, like a mountain covered with snow; for, as to those parts of it that were not gilt, they were exceedingly white" (Josephus *War* 5.5.6).

APPENDIX D

References to Mark in the New Testament

"When he realized this, he went to the house of Mary, the mother of John Mark" (Acts 12:12).

"And Barnabas and Saul returned to Jerusalem after they had completed their relief mission, on which they took John Mark" (Acts 12:25).

"Arriving in Salamis, they proclaimed God's message in the Jewish synagogues. They also had John as their assistant" (Acts 13:5).

"Paul and his companions set sail from Paphos and came to Perga in Pamphylia. John, however, left them and went back to Jerusalem" (Acts 13:13).

"Barnabas wanted to take along John Mark. But Paul did not think it appropriate to take along this man who had deserted them in Pamphylia and had not gone on with them to the work. There was such a sharp disagreement that they parted company, and Barnabas took Mark with him and sailed off to Cyprus" (Acts 15:37-39).

"Aristarchus, my fellow prisoner, greets you, as does Mark, Barnabas' cousin (concerning whom you have received instructions: if he comes to you, welcome him)" (Col 4:10).

"Epaphras, my fellow prisoner in Christ Jesus, greets you, and so do Mark, Aristarchus, Demas, and Luke, my co-workers" (Philem 23-24).

"Only Luke is with me. Bring Mark with you, for he is useful to me in the ministry" (2 Tim 4:11).

"She who is in Babylon, also chosen, sends you greetings, as does Mark, my son" (1 Pet 5:13).

APPENDIX E

The Additional Ending of Mark

*T*his is a brief overview of the basic issues regarding the later additions to Mark's Gospel. I chose to present the information here, as opposed to the body of the commentary, because my desire is to interact with the text and not become mired in the issue. This is a sensitive subject for those of us who believe deeply in biblical authority. It is my deep conviction that a discerning approach to the reliability of a passage such as this, which is clearly secondary to the original, is to take the authority of Scripture profoundly seriously. A serious study of the various texts and their different levels of reliability calls for an entire book-sized study of its own. For an exhaustive look at variant readings and the different textual issues, I encourage you to look at William Lane's *The Gospel of Mark* in the New International Commentary on the New Testament (Eerdmans, 1974). The following notes are an edited version of those provided by Bill in the last class he taught on Mark for our church.

1. Textual evidence supports the conclusion that Mark ended his Gospel at Mark 16:8. The evidence includes:
   a. The two earliest complete copies of Mark in Greek end with 16:8.
   b. An important Old Latin version ends with 16:8.
   c. The Old Syriac version as well as the two most important Georgian versions end with 16:8.
   d. The church fathers Clement of Alexandria, Origen, Cyprian, and Cyril of Jerusalem show no awareness of Mark 16:9-20.
   e. Eusebius (fourth century) states that "accurate" copies of Mark end with 16:8.

    f. Jerome (fifth century) echoes this testimony. He states that almost all Greek codices do not contain Mark 16:9-20.

2. The literary evidence of style and vocabulary, based on comparison with Mark 1:1–16:8, shows that Mark 16:9-20 is not consistent with Markan authorship.

3. Both Matthew and Luke follow Mark until 16:8. There they diverge completely.

4. The transition from Mark 16:8 to 16:9 is awkward. The subject of 16:8 is the women; the presumed subject of 16:9 is Jesus.

5. The form, language and style of 16:9-20 show that Mark did not compose this portion of the text. Its origin can be traced to the early second century when it was noticed that Mark appeared to be incomplete because the Gospel did not report any appearances by the risen Lord.

6. The response of the women to the evidence of God's decisive intervention in raising Jesus from the dead is described by Mark as terror (Mk 16:8). The cause of the women's fear is the presence and action of God at the tomb of Jesus. The first human response is overwhelming fear. Mark 16:9-20 seems to contradict this reaction.

NOTES

[1]Cited by William Lane, *Mark*, The New International Commentary on the New Testament (Grand Rapids: Eerdmans, 1974), p. 43.

[2]Michael Green, *The Message of Matthew* (Downers Grove, Ill.: InterVarsity Press, 1988), p. 85.

[3]Geza Vermes, *Who's Who in the Age of Jesus* (New York: Penguin Reference Library, 2005), pp. 83-85.

[4]Webb Mealy, *The Spoken English New Testament: A New Translation from the Greek* (Oakland, Calif.: Sent Press, 2008), p. 95.

[5]For an interesting discussion of this see R. Alan Cole, *Mark*, Tyndale New Testament Commentaries (Downers Grove, Ill.: IVP Academic, 1961), pp. 138-40.

[6]Xavier Leon-Dufour, *Dictionary of the New Testament* (San Francisco: Harper and Row, 1980), p. 111.

[7]For Salome see Cole, *Mark*, p. 177, and Vermes, *Who's Who*, p. 221. For Herod and Herodias see Vermes, *Who's Who*, pp. 47-48, 111.

[8]The complete absence of miracle language has led some liberal scholars to conclude that, in fact, no miracle occurred—it was simply a matter of the crowd witnessing the generosity of the young boy and following his example. See William Barclay, *The Gospel of Luke* (Louisville, Ky.: Westminster John Knox, 1975), p. 140.

[9]In Hebrew the leftovers were called the *peah* and were collected after the meal and given to the slaves.

[10]R. Laird Harris, *Theological Wordbook of the Old Testament* (Chicago: Moody Press, 1980), 2:813.

[11]Here is the parallel structure of the feeding miracles: Miracle of feeding (Mk 6:31-44; 8:1-8); coming to the other side (Mk 6:45-56; 8:10); confrontation with Pharisees (Mk 7:1-23; 8:11-13); misunderstanding about bread (Mk 7:24-30; 8:13-21); healings (Mk 7:31-36; 8:22-26); conclusion about Jesus (Mk 7:37; 8:27-30).

[12]Eusebius, *Eusebius: The Church History*, trans. Paul L. Maier (Grand Rapids: Kregel, 1999), p. 110.

[13]Cited by Lane, *Mark*, p. 394.

[14]Lane, *Mark*, p. 405.

[15]Clint E. Arnold, *Illustrated Bible Backgrounds Commentary* (Grand Rapids: Zondervan, 2002), 1:270.

[16]There are no references to the temple market (sometimes referred to as "the bazaar of Annas") being moved from the Mount of Olives to the temple court before A.D.

30, when John records Jesus' first expulsion of the traders. Perhaps Jesus' initial anger is a reflection of seeing the market in the temple precincts for the first time.

[17]Leon-Dufour, *Dictionary*, p. 358

[18]Cited by Arnold, *Illustrated Bible Backgrounds*, 1.277.

[19]Eusebius, *Church History*, p. 95.

[20]Is this the same incident recorded by John in 12:1-8? The locations may be the same. Mark places the event at the home of "Simon the Leper." In John no specific location is given, only that Martha is serving while Lazarus is reclining with Jesus (Jn 12:2). In John's account Mary is identified by name. In Mark the woman is nameless. In John, Mary anoints Jesus' feet, while the nameless woman in Mark anoints his head. Mark records Jesus' memorializing her gift (as does Matthew [Mt 26:13]).

[21]Peter's companion Paul no doubt heard from his close associate that Jesus used this intimate name for his Father. Paul goes on to embrace that same intimacy for us in Romans 8:15 and Galatians 4:6.

[22]George Martin, *Bringing the Gospel of Mark to Life* (Ijamsville, Md.: The Word Among Us Press, 2005), p. 415.

[23]Arnold, *Illustrated Bible Backgrounds*, pp. 294-95.

[24]Leon-Dufour, *Dictionary*, p. 324.

[25]Josephus, *Josephus: The Complete Works*, trans. William Whiston (Grand Rapids: Kregel, 1960), p. 500.

[26]Tacitus *Annals* 6.29.

RESOURCES

Barnett, Paul. *The Birth of Christianity: The First Twenty Years.* Grand Rapids: Eerdmans, 2005.

Barrett, C. K. *The New Testament Background: Selected Documents.* New York: Harper and Row, 1987.

Bell, Albert A. *Exploring the New Testament World.* Nashville: Thomas Nelson, 1998.

Boring, M. Eugene, Klaus Berger and Carsten Colpe. *Hellenistic Commentary to the New Testament.* Nashville: Abingdon, 1995.

Bruce, F. F. *New Testament History.* Garden City, N.Y.: Doubleday Galilee, 1972.

Connolly, Peter. *Living in the Time of Jesus of Nazareth.* Oxford: Oxford University Press, 1983.

Dando-Collins, Stephen. *The Great Fire of Rome.* Cambridge, Mass.: Da Capo Press, 2010.

Donfried, Karl, and Peter Richardson, eds. *Judaism and Christianity in First Century Rome.* Grand Rapids: Eerdmans, 1998.

Grant, Michael. *The Roman Emperors.* New York: Barnes and Noble, 1985.

Guelich, Robert A. *Mark.* Word Biblical Commentary. Nashville: Thomas Nelson, 1989.

Kernaghan, Ronald J. *Mark.* IVP New Testament Commentary. Downers Grove, Ill.: InterVarsity Press, 2007.

Lawrence, Paul. *The IVP Atlas of the Bible.* Downers Grove, Ill.: IVP Academic, 2006.

McReynolds, Paul R. *Word Study Greek-English New Testament.* Wheaton, Ill.: Tyndale House, 1966.

Meeks, Wayne A. *The First Urban Christians.* New Haven, Conn.: Yale University Press, 1983.

Oden, Thomas C., ed. *Mark.* Ancient Christian Commentary on Scripture. Downers Grove, Ill.: InterVarsity Press, 1998.

Pliny the Younger. *Complete Letters.* Translated by P. G. Walsh. Oxford: Oxford University Press, 2006.

Saldarini, Anthony J. *Pharisees, Scribes and Sadducees in Palestinian Society.* Grand Rapids: Eerdmans, 1988.

Scott, J. Julius. *Jewish Backgrounds of the New Testament.* Grand Rapids: Baker, 1995.

Suetonius. *The Twelve Caesars.* Translated by Robert Graves. New York: Penguin Classics, 1982.

Tacitus. *The Annals of Rome.* Translated by Michael Grant. New York: Penguin Classics, 1996.

Throckmorton, Burton H. *Gospel Parallels.* Nashville: Thomas Nelson, 1967.

Wilken, Robert L. *The Christians as the Romans Saw Them.* New Haven, Conn.: Yale University Press, 1984.

ABOUT THE AUTHOR

For many years Michael Card has struggled to listen to the Scripture at the level of his imagination. The result has been thirty-two albums and twenty-three books, all examining a different element of the Bible, from the life of the apostle Peter to slavery in the New Testament to Christ-centered creativity.

He has a master's degree in biblical studies from Western Kentucky University as well as honorary Ph.D.s in music (Whitfield Seminary) and Christian education (Philadelphia Biblical University).

He lives with his wife, Susan, and their four children in Franklin, Tennessee, where together they pursue racial reconciliation and neighborhood renewal.

www.michaelcard.com

ABOUT THE BIBLICAL IMAGINATION SERIES

The Biblical Imagination Series is made up of four elements: commentary, music, on-site experience and community discussion. The series will overview the Gospels by means of a commentary on each of the four books, a collection of songs and a video teaching series from Israel as well as a touring conference series. For more information go to the Facebook page for "Biblical Imagination with Michael Card" or visit

www.biblicalimagination.com

Now Available:
Mark: *The Gospel of Passion*
Luke: *The Gospel of Amazement*

Forthcoming:
Matthew: *The Gospel of Fulfillment (2013)*
John: *The Gospel of Wisdom (2014)*

ALSO AVAILABLE FROM INTERVARSITY PRESS:

Mark: *The Heartfelt Fervor of Jesus*
music CD
ISBN: 978-0-8308-3802-8

Luke: *A World Turned Upside Down*
music CD
ISBN: 978-0-8308-3801-1

Scribbling in the Sand: *Christ and Creativity*
168 pages, paperback
ISBN: 978-0-8308-3254-5

A Fragile Stone: *The Emotional Life of Simon Peter*
192 pages, paperback
ISBN: 978-0-8308-3445-7

A Better Freedom: *Finding Life as Slaves of Christ*
168 pages, paperback
ISBN: 978-0-8308-3714-4